C0-BXA-860

The Doctrines of Heathen Philosophy

(1804)

By Joseph Priestley

A PHOTOREPRODUCTION
WITH AN INTRODUCTION BY
TERENCE ALLAN HOAGWOOD

SCHOLARS' FACSIMILES & REPRINTS
DELMAR, NEW YORK, 1987

SCHOLARS' FACSIMILES & REPRINTS
ISSN 0161-7729
SERIES ESTABLISHED 1936
VOLUME 426

Published by Scholars' Facsimiles & Reprints
Delmar, New York 12054-0344, U.S.A.

Reproduced from a copy in
and with the permission of
The New York University Libraries

Library of Congress Cataloging-in-Publication Data

Priestley, Joseph, 1733-1804.

[The doctrines of heathen philosophy compared with those of revelation]
The doctrines of heathen philosophy (1804) /
by Joseph Priestley ; a photoreproduction
with an introduction by Terence Allan Hoagwood.
p. cm. –
(Scholars' Facsimiles & Reprints, ISSN 0161-7729 ; v. 426)
Reprint. Originally published: The doctrines
of heathen philosophy compared with those of revelation. 1804.
ISBN 0-8201-1426-X
1. Christianity and other religions–Greek.
2. Christianity and other religions–Roman.
3. Revelation. 4. Philosophy, Ancient.
5. Philosophy and religion.
6. Unitarian Universalist churches–Doctrines.
I. Title.
BR128.A2P8 1987
261.5'1–dc 19 87-26848
CIP

Introduction

"As a controversialist, no man upon record has been more distinguished than Dr. Priestley"; so says the anonymous obituary of Priestley that appeared in *The Gentleman's Magazine* [74 (1804): 378], and certainly Priestley was one of the most prolific writers of polemical books who ever lived. Incurring governmental pressure and threats, and even mob violence, Priestley left England in 1794, having published works of the first rank in political argument, theology, physical science, and philosophy. Upon his departure he published the politically inflammatory *Present State of Europe Compared with Ancient Prophecies: A Sermon* with a "Farewell Discourse" containing "Reasons for the Author's Leaving England" (London: J. Johnson, 1794). Those reasons concern oppression, bigotry, and real personal and political danger. During the most dramatically revolutionary period of European history Priestley was a leading champion of the radical dissent that celebrated and sought to extend the principles of the French revolution. Accordingly, he was venerated, loved, hated, and feared.

There is little question, however, that the political causes united with some matters of temperament to produce and to maintain Priestley's contentious position. His method was often disputative and confrontational, and his topics were among the most hotly disputed. One example will suffice to illustrate Priestley's polemical habits: his enormously influential *History of the Corruptions of Christianity* appeared in 1782 (London: J. Johnson); it then reappeared in a series beginning in the following year, to include "A Reply to the Animadversions in the *Monthly Review*"; he added "Letters to Mr. Horsley [a hostile critic of Priestley], Part 1"; the *Monthly Review* replied to these defenses, and Priestley published all the disputation together with the original text of the *History*. He then followed this desperately contested argument with another in support of it, *An History of Early Opinions concerning Jesus Christ* (Birmingham: Printed by Pearson and Rollason and sold by J. Johnson, London, 1786). This book was in turn met with replies and animadversions, and of course Priestley kept on replying and adding to the controversy for the rest of his long and productive life. His *Present*

State of Europe lists seventy-seven of his books published already by 1794, and he wrote another dozen volumes after he subsequently arrived in America.

Priestley's influential volumes were all intensely controversial: for example, his *Letters to a Philosophical Unbeliever* (Bath: Printed by R. Cruttwell and sold by J. Johnson, London, 1780) was initially an argument against Hume; in 1787 he added to this volume an argument with Gibbon; and in 1795, an argument with Paine. These polemical examples could easily be multiplied, and for Priestley more than for most writers it can be said that his books come close to constituting his life. Collectively, Priestley's works in science, political theory, philosophy, and theology provide the context for his last book, *Doctrines of Heathen Philosophy Compared with Those of Revelation*, the masterpiece of intellectual history that is here reprinted.

"As an experimental Philosopher, he was, perhaps, the very first of his age" (*Gentleman's Magazine* 74 [1804]: 378), according to a contemporary. The same reviewer, however, regrets Priestley's "political and theological writings" as "fraught with principles the most destructive to the well-being of society" (p. 378). Such a dichotomy between Priestley's science and his political or theological thought, however, is not finally tenable; conceptually his work is unified. He did make several specific and original contributions (including the isolation of oxygen, of ammonia, of sulfur dioxide, nitrous oxide, and nitrogen dioxide; the discovery of the function of the blood in respiration; the contrivance of artificially carbonated water; the initial work toward discovering and analyzing photosynthesis; and many others[1]), but Priestley's work is more importantly and consistently theoretical. Its central effort is a unification of apparently separate elements, substances, or systems, or rather an articulation of the ground of their unity and coherence. At the highest cognitive level this paradigm of unification also informs his philosophical works and especially the *Doctrines of Heathen Philosophy Compared with Those of Revelation*.

In his first scientific work (*History and Present State of Electricity* [London: Printed for J. Dodsley, J. Johnson and B. Davenport, and T. Cadell, 1767]), Priestley relates past and current discoveries, and for the first time he produces a scale of conductivity as a common property of different substances. He also discovers the unified inverse-square form of the law of force obtaining between electrical charges. The theory articulated in his *History and Present State of Discoveries Relating to Vision, Light, and Colours* (London: J. Johnson, 1772) transcends the old dualism of ether and particles, and then goes farther, unifying substance and light, matter and motion, by redefining the supposed dichotomy as two forms of the one reality.

Priestley's best-known scientific accomplishment is the discovery of oxygen, announced in his "Account of Further Observations on Air" (*Philosophical Transactions of the Royal Society* for 1775). There is no denying the persistence with which Priestley clung to his theory of phlogiston to misconstrue this discovery: he posited phlogiston as a hypothetical and universal substance essential to fire and life. When he succeeded in experimentally isolating oxygen for the first time in human history, he interpreted the gas as "dephlogisticated air"–that is, normal air from which all the phlogiston had been removed. This explanation did accord with his comprehensive theory, though it prevented the correct identification of the gas, and Priestley persisted in it from 1774 when he first exhibited the gas to Lavoisier, until his death thirty years later, when he was still disputing the point.

Two volumes bring Priestley's scientific work into explicit unity with his theological and philosophical arguments: his *Doctrine of Philosophical Necessity, Illustrated* and *Disquisitions Relating to Matter and Spirit* (both published in 1777). Here Priestley explains monism, the paradigm of unification that appears recurrently in his later philosophical work: "The notion of two substances that have no common property, and yet are capable of intimate connection and mutual action, is both absurd and modern; a substance without extension or relation to place being unknown both in the Scriptures, and to all antiquity."[2] To the orthodox dualisms of body/soul, spirit/mind, matter/energy, Priestley opposes a principle of essential union, and in the context of philosophical history that is the burden too of *Doctrines of Heathen Philosophy Compared with Those of Revelation*.

When Thomas Jefferson was asked to recommend a course of study for his young friend James Madison, one of the authors of political philosophy whom Jefferson advised Madison to read was Priestley.[3] Priestley's first book of political philosophy is *An Essay on the First Principles of Government: On the Nature of Political, Civil, and Religious Liberty* (London: Printed for J. Dodsley, T. Cadell, and J. Johnson, 1768). Its influence was extraordinary: this book is the origin of Jeremy Bentham's "utilitarian principle"–that is, the rule of right as "the greatest good for the greatest number." In the following year Priestley published a volume on the legality of dissent (*Remarks on Some Paragraphs in . . . Dr. Blackstone's Commentaries on the*

Laws of England, Relating to the Dissenters [London: J. Johnson and J. Payne, 1769]). By 1775, on the verge of the American Revolution, Benjamin Franklin was consulting with Priestley. Together they interpreted political news, as Franklin's peace-seeking mission in London came to its unsuccessful end; within weeks the fighting erupted in Lexington.[4]

To the more conservative, Priestley appeared, predictably, a "turbulent, seditious man"; a contemporary reports that "his pulpit discourses, his political pamphlets, and his private conversation, were well known to be highly inimical to the Government of his country, and especially to her Ecclesiastical Constitution" (*Gentleman's Magazine* 74 [1804]: 375). That same offended Government intimated more than once that Priestley should leave England, and for obvious reasons, given his support of the democratic movements in America and France, while the increasingly reactionary British government intensified its oppressions at home.

In 1789, the year the French revolution began, Priestley preached against the Test and the Corporation Acts, which barred dissenters from public life; a series of attacks and persistent defenses ensued. In 1791 Priestley published *Letters to the Right Honourable Edmund Burke, Occasioned by His Reflections on the Revolutions in France* (of which Joseph Johnson was already publishing a third edition in the same year). Here he celebrates that which his monarch and his monarch's ministers most feared: political revolution meant to "make a totally new, a most wonderful, and important, aera in the history of mankind . . . a liberating of all the powers of man."[5] Reaction was swift: a Church-and-King mob burned Priestley's house in Birmingham, destroying his library and experimental equipment and threatening his life.[6]

The controversy that included Burke's *Reflections* and the famous replies–first Mary Wollstonecraft's *Vindication of the Rights of Men* (also published by Joseph Johnson, in 1790), then Priestley's *Letters to . . . Burke* in 1791, and then Paine's *Rights of Man* in 1791-92–were neither political nor religious, but always essentially both; by his contemporaries Priestley was viewed as "the most dangerous enemy of the established religion, in its connection with the state."[7] As a narrowly political discrimination along exactly religious lines, the notorious Test and Corporation Acts were as thorough an interweaving of those two contexts as were Priestley's powerful polemics against them.

After the Birmingham riots Priestley took up residence in London, but what Chalmers calls prejudice and hostility met him there. The Royal Society, of which he had been a Fellow for twenty-five years, snubbed him; Priestley's published appeals to such radical groups as the Friends of the Constitution (in France), and to the Academy of Science at Paris (whose secretary was the prominent revolutionist Condorcet), inflamed English authorities (see Chalmers, p. 304). Priestley's friends expressed fear that he would suffer the fate of the numerous arrested radicals in the reactionary period and encouraged his flight. Accordingly, Priestley sailed for America in 1794, leaving behind a record of his reasons and taking with him both international fame and also some massive current projects, primarily theological, to which he wished to dedicate the remainder of his life (Edgar F. Smith, *Priestley in America, 1794-1804* [1920; rpt. New York: Arno Press, 1980], p. 53).

He was greeted by welcoming addresses of learned and civic associations and by published announcements honoring him. Unanimously these announcements praise Priestley as a foe to bigotry and tyranny and as a world leader in the defense of free inquiry and the extension of liberty in all its forms (Smith, *Priestley in America*, pp. 12-33). Among his acquaintances (and in his audiences when he lectured and preached) were Thomas Jefferson and John Adams,[8] and on the religious thought of both of these Americans the *Doctrines of Heathen Philosophy Compared with Those of Revelation* was to have important influence.

Controversy, however, persisted in Priestley's life: in 1798, fearful perhaps of the supporters of the French during the rising hostility and likely war with France, Adams's administration instituted the Alien and Sedition Acts, whereby radicals of the French school could be deported (see Haraszti, *John Adams & the Prophets of Progress*, p. 281). Timothy Pickering, Adams's secretary of state, wanted specifically to deport Priestley (see Lindsay, in *Autobiography of Joseph Priestley*, p. 32). Adams's letters reveal that the issues were philosophical as well as narrowly political: Adams correctly associated Priestley's theories of perfectibility with French-style radicals and specifically Condorcet.[9] Condorcet's *Esquisse d'un Tableau historique des progrès de l'esprit humain* (Paris: Agasse, an III [1795]) was a primary source on this theory, and so were Priestley's *Essay on the First Principles of Government* and William Godwin's *Political Justice*. But as Adams knew, the relevant notions reappear in a new and theological context in the *Doctrines of Heathen Philosophy*.

While Adams did not in fact allow the deportation of Priestley,

Thomas Cooper, who helped Priestley with revisions associated with *Doctrines of Heathen Philosophy*, was imprisoned. Not until Jefferson's election in 1800, Priestley was to say, did he ever in his life find himself in a country whose political authorities were friendly to him (see Schofield, "Priestley," 11: 141). The affinity of Jefferson and Priestley was in large measure a philosophical matter: their friendship and correspondence gave rise specifically to the book here reprinted, for example, to whose history and place in Priestley's theological corpus I therefore now turn.

The philosophical and political character of Adams's response to Priestley is a matter of clear documentary record: that response, like Jefferson's praise, focuses on the religious issues that come to final expression in the compendious *Doctrines of Heathen Philosophy*. Adams had met Priestley in London; later he attended Priestley's Unitarian chapel sermons, and he attended also Priestley's lectures, "The Evidences of Revealed Religion" (Haraszti, pp. 280-81). Priestley dedicated the published volume of those lectures to Adams; the relatively conservative recipient of this honor expressed privately his fear that this much association with Priestley "will get me the character of a heretic." Adams stopped attending Priestley's lectures, and the outright political hostility toward him opened subsequently.

By this time, however, Priestley's influence had left its mark, having convinced Adams, for example, of the value of much ancient literature, even in comparison with Hebrew scriptures. Adams wrote responses to Priestley's *Doctrines of Heathen Philosophy* (Haraszti, pp. 289-90), so the two men's differences are easily identified. Similarly expressive are the two men's statements about Plato (see Haraszti, pp. 286-87, and below, pp. 121ff.). After Priestley's death Adams wrote to Jefferson about this "learned, indefatigable, most excellent and extraordinary man,"[10] and Adams said of *Doctrines of Heathen Philosophy*, "I regret, oh how I lament that he did not live to publish this work! It must exist in manuscript. Cooper must know something of it. Can you learn where it is, and get it printed?"

Adams acquired his copy of this book from Jefferson, and Jefferson's agency in this respect is significant: the heart of this volume is the essay, "Socrates and Jesus Compared," which Priestley had published separately in 1803; Jefferson wrote enthusiastically to Priestley about this work, encouraging him both to publish defenses augmenting his argument and also to expand the work by adding comparisons with other ancient philosophers and systems, including

Epicurus and Seneca.[11] Priestley did exactly that (see below, pp. 240-76), and the result is the present volume. It is also true, as Sanford says, that Jefferson also produced a small start at such a comparison, after Priestley's "Socrates and Jesus Compared" (see *The Writings of Thomas Jefferson*, 10: 381-85). Sanford, however, is evidently unaware of Priestley's book, of which Jefferson's is derivative.[12]

Jefferson and Priestley agree almost entirely on many points expressed in the *Doctrines of Heathen Philosophy*–the belief that the doctrine of the Trinity is an impertinence derived from Platonism (see Sanford, *The Religious Life of Thomas Jefferson*, pp. 88, 112; and *The Writings of Thomas Jefferson*, 10: 384), the rejection of the worship of Mary and the saints, and the denial of the unique divinity of Jesus Christ (see *The Writings of Thomas Jefferson*, 10: 380). Priestley's *Institutes of Natural and Revealed Religion* (3 vols., London: J. Johnson, 1772-74) is his first thorough exploration of this argument.[13]

Important differences between Jefferson and Priestley also warrant analysis (concerning the nature or reality of providence, for example), but the most general affinity in this connection is their shared sympathy with the humanistic syncretism that arose in the renaissance but flourished in the eighteenth century. As Jean Seznec says, this scholarly movement gave rise to the idea "that all religions have the same worth, and that under their varied forms . . . is hidden a common truth."[14] Albert J. Kuhn has said that, in the analysis and comparison of mythological systems and texts, deists "hoped to find evidence for their central idea of a theology which was at once natural, simple, and universal" (p. 1103). *The Doctrines of Heathen Philosophy* makes it clear that Priestley was no deist in the narrowest of the eighteenth-century senses of that term:[15] he insists repeatedly and forcibly, in this volume and in his *Memoirs*, on the constant action and intervention of an engaged providence; but his work nonetheless shares that aim of natural and universal theology. (The definition of "deism" that Jefferson worked out, when he was practically collaborating with Priestley, certainly would include both of these thinkers: "Deism; that is, the belief in one only God" [*The Writings of Thomas Jefferson*, 10: 382]. This "deism" is unitarianism in a nutshell, and Priestley is perhaps the most vigorously outspoken Unitarian in history.)

Priestley's most controversial theological positions reappear from his earlier works in the present volume: he had founded the *Theological Repository* in 1767, largely to advance his "objections to the doctrine of the miraculous conception of Jesus, and his natural fallibility and peccability" (*Autobiography*, p. 121), and of course his denial of the divinity of Jesus is an argument of other volumes as well. His doubts about the immateriality of the soul (and these doubts constitute "obnoxious sentiments," according to Chalmers in 1812 [p. 303]) inform his *Disquisitions Relating to Matter and Spirit* as well as his writings on Christianity; but his aims in the *Doctrines of Heathen Philosophy* involve an urgent and humane practicality, rather than a theological disputation. The human moral value and force of the philosophers and of scripture concern him here, and not (as he insists repeatedly) their metaphysics. Movingly, Priestley here deepens his argument with a pathos and emotional honesty that he does not often allow himself elsewhere (as in his comments on the emotional force of the Psalms).

That pathos is enhanced for us by the facts surrounding this book's composition (see *Autobiography*, pp. 135-36; *Gentleman's Magazine*, 74: 378-79): he knew that he was dying, but he managed to hold on until he was satisfied with the last revisions. He died within forty minutes of seeing his last corrections (concerning the central essay, "Socrates and Jesus Compared") entered properly. In his own words, "I could not have closed my life with more satisfaction than after a work of this kind" (p. xii, below). And exactly here his life does in fact close. Priestley's discourses on death—honest, perceptive, but surprisingly optimistic (see, e.g., pp. 225-26, below)—are invested with special importance by their context in his life, as the culmination and last word, literally as well as conceptually, of the philosopher's life.

The work is not wholly unprecedented: Priestley had written *A Comparison of the Institutions of Moses with Those of the Hindoos and Other Nations; with Remarks on Mr. Dupuis's "Origin of All Religions"* . . . (Northumberland: A. Kennedy, 1799), and then *An Inquiry into the Knowledge of the Ancient Hebrews Concerning a Future State* (London: J. Johnson, 1801). Dupuis's antecedent volume is a work of comparative religion, published posthumously; Dupuis was another associate of Condorcet and a member of the French National Convention, which had offered Priestley membership as well (see *Gentleman's Magazine*, 62 [1792]: 947). In English, Edward Stillingfleet had argued (as Priestley does here) for the superior certainty of Moses's knowledge, in comparison with pagan's uncertainty; for the evidence of miracles; against the atheist tendency of both Aristotle and Epicurus; and about the corruption among the pagans of ancient truths, in a process of doctrinal deterioration.[16]

John Toland had written, as Priestley does here, a history of the heathen concepts of the soul's immortality, with an argument (also like Priestley's) that motion is essential to matter.[17] And Theophilus Gale had published in 1672 a study of pagan philosophy and literature, arguing as Priestley does in this book for the moral priority of scripture and for the derivative quality of Homer and Hesiod in particular; Gale also compares with scripture the doctrines of Socrates, Plato, Aristotle, the Stoics, and the Epicureans.[18] But the principles, purposes, and emphases of Priestley are very different from those of his relatively orthodox and uniformly dualistic predecessors.

Doctrines of Heathen Philosophy contains, then, analyses of the philosophical (and primarily ethical) systems of Pythagoras, Socrates, Plato, Aristotle, the Stoics (Marcus [Aurelius] Antoninus and Epictetus), Arrian, Seneca, and Epicurus. He treats these philosophers always in comparison with scriptural doctrines. These comparisons tend often to take a three-part conceptual form, though never formally or mechanically: (1) Priestley typically offers an exposition of elements in the particular system which he finds enduringly valuable; (2) he discerns a moral priority for scriptural teaching, though not for orthodox doctrine; this superiority usually involves providence as a divine invasion of the human world, or it involves a concept of material immortality, or both; and (3) Priestley constructs an argument on the deep-level conceptual harmony of the philosophical systems. In magisterial clarity Priestley articulates an amicable accord for apparently antagonistic schools of thought.

As one of Priestley's distinguished followers was to say, "I can conceive a great work, embodying the discoveries of all ages, & harmonizing the contending creeds by which mankind have been ruled."[19] Priestley's life's work is designed to be that great work; this book is its final statement, and Priestley's last word.

TERENCE ALLAN HOAGWOOD

Texas A & M University

NOTES

1. Robert Schofield, "Priestley," in *Dictionary of Scientific Biography*, ed. Charles Coulston Gillespie (New York: Charles Scribner's Sons, 1975). See also Schofield's commentary in *A Scientific Autobiography of Joseph Priestley* (Cambridge, MA: M.I.T. Press, 1963).

2. Priestley, *Disquisitions Relating to Matter and Spirit*, 2d ed. (London: Printed by Pearson and Rollason for J. Johnson, 1787), 1: iii. Obviously Priestley shares this idea with the French Encyclopedists, with whose thought and work he was deeply familiar and often sympathetic. See Jack Lindsay's learned essay, printed as an introduction to *Autobiography of Joseph Priestley* (Bath: Adams and Dart, 1970), p. 22; Terence Allan Hoagwood, *Prophecy and the Philosophy of Mind* (University, AL: University of Alabama Press, 1985), p. 35; and, for a comparison of Priestley in this connection with one of the major poets among his acquaintances, Hoagwood, "Holbach and Blake's Philosophical Statement in 'The Voice of the Devil,'" *English Language Notes*, 15 (1978), 181-86.

3. See James Parton, *Life of Thomas Jefferson* (1874; rpt. New York: Da Capo Press, 1971), p. 61.

4. See Catherine Drinker Bowen, *John Adams and the American Revolution* (Boston: Little, Brown and Co., 1950), p. 517; and Priestley, *Autobiography*, p. 117. This volume entitled *Autobiography* is a reprint of *Memoirs of Joseph Priestley, to the Year 1795, Written by Himself; with a Continuation, to the Time of His Decease, by His Son, Joseph Priestley, and Observations on His Writings, by Thomas Cooper . . . and the Rev. William Christie* (Northumberland: John Binns, 1806; London: J. Johnson, 1806), to which Lindsay has added his essay as introduction.

5. Priestley, *Letters to the Right Honourable Edmund Burke . . .*, 3rd ed. (London: J. Johnson, 1791), pp. 143-44.

6. See *Gentleman's Magazine*, 74 (1804): 375; Priestley, *Autobiography*, pp. 129-31; and Priestley, *An Appeal to the Public, on the Subject of the Riots in Birmingham* (Birmingham: Printed by J. Thompson and sold by J. Johnson, London, 1791).

7. "Priestley," in *The General Biographical Dictionary: Containing an Historical and Critical Account of the Lives and Writings of the Most Eminent Persons in Every Nation; Particularly, the British and the Irish; from the Earliest Accounts to the Present Time*, rev. ed. by

Alexander Chalmers (London: J. Nichols and others, 1812), 25: 303.

8. See Parton, *Life of Thomas Jefferson*, p. 530; Charles B. Sanford, *The Religious Life of Thomas Jefferson* (Charlottesville, VA: University Press of Virginia, 1984), p. 112; and Zoltan Haraszti, *John Adams and the Prophets of Progress* (Cambridge, MA: Harvard University Press, 1952), pp. 280-81.

9. See *The Founding Fathers: John Adams in His Own Words*, ed. James Bishop Peabody (New York: Harper & Row, 1973), p. 388.

10. Adams's remark appears in a letter to Jefferson: *The Writings of Thomas Jefferson*, ed. Andrew A. Lipscomb and Albert Ellery Bergh (Washington, DC: The Thomas Jefferson Memorial Association, 1904), 13:323.

11. See Smith, *Priestley in America*, p. 156; and Sanford, *The Religious Life of Thomas Jefferson*, p. 102.

12. Sanford, *The Religious Life of Thomas Jefferson*, p. 102. Karl Lehmann acknowledges the importance of this project that Priestley planned, but seems similarly to have overlooked the fact that Priestley did in fact write the book: see Lehmann, *Thomas Jefferson: American Humanist* (Charlottesville, VA: University Press of Virginia, 1985), p. 63: "After the death of the Unitarian Priestley, who had published a comparison of the doctrines of Jesus and Socrates and had promised to extend that comparison to the other ancient schools of philosophy, Jefferson resumed these studies himself. . . ."

13. Relevant arguments constitute also the burden of Priestley's *An History of the Corruptions of Christianity* in 1782 and *An History of Early Opinions Concerning Jesus Christ . . . Proving that the Christian Church Was at First Unitarian* in 1786.

14. Seznec, *The Survival of the Pagan Gods* (New York: Bollingen, 1953), p. 98. On this syncretic movement see also Albert J. Kuhn, "English Deism and the Development of Romantic Mythological Syncretism," *PMLA*, 71 (1956), 1094-1116.

15. In 1705 Samuel Clarke published an argument in which he distinguishes four kinds of deists; those who deny providence make up one variety, and this is the narrow sense of the word "deist" which would exclude Priestley. See Clarke's *A Demonstration of the Being and Attributes of God* (London: J. Knapton, 1705). On this point of definition, see also Ernest Campbell Mossner, "Deism," in *Encyclopedia of Philosophy*, ed. Paul Edwards (1967; rpt. New York: Macmillan, 1972), 2: 326-36.

16. Edward Stillingfleet, *Origines Sacrae*, 4th ed. (London: Henry

Mortlock, 1675), pp. 73, 107, 252, 360-420, and 557-98.

17. Toland, *Letters to Serena* (London: Bernard Lintot, 1704), pp. 19-68.

18. Gale, *The Court of the Gentiles*, 2d ed. (Oxon: Tho. Gilbert, 1672), Part I, Book iii (paginated separately), 7-8; Part II, pp. 222, 235, 248-49, 317, 422, 497, and 512.

19. Percy Bysshe Shelley, *Letters*, ed. Frederick L. Jones (Oxford: Oxford University Press, 1964), 2: 70-71.

THE DOCTRINES

of

HEATHEN PHILOSOPHY,

compared

WITH THOSE OF

REVELATION

BY JOSEPH PRIESTLEY, L. L. D. F. R. S.

Northumberland:
PRINTED BY JOHN BINNS.
....
1804.
....

DEDICATION.

TO THE

REVEREND JOSEPH BERINGTON,

a Catholic Priest in England,

AND TO THE

RIGHT REVEREND WILLIAM WHITE,

a Bishop of the Episcopalian Church in the United States.

GENTLEMEN,

YOU will, I doubt not, be surprized at my dedication of any work of mine to you, differing so much as we do in our sentiments concerning christianity. But, entertaining the highest respect for your characters, as men and as christians, I do it *because* we differ; to shew, with respect to a subject in which we are equally interested, as in that of this work that I regard all that bear the christian name, how widely distant soever their different churches and creeds may be, as friends and brethren, and therefore entitled, by the express direction of our common Saviour, to particular respect and attention as such.

Though few persons have written more than myself to controvert the established principles of each of your churches, I consider the articles in which we all agree as of infinitely more moment than those with respect to which we differ. We all believe in the being, the perfections, the universal providence, and the righteous moral government of God, as the maker and sovereign disposer of all things. Whatever we may think of the person of Christ, we all believe that his doctrine is divine, and his precepts obligatory upon all. We all believe in his miracles, his death, his resurrection, and his ascension, as related in the books of the New Testament. We also all believe that he will come again, to raise all the dead, to judge the world, and to give to every man according to his works; and these are all the articles of faith that can have any considerable influence on the lives and conduct of men. Believing this, our gratitude for the communication of knowledge of such infinite importance must be common to us all, and such as should

lead

lead to a chearful obedience to all the commands of God.

I know that the creeds of both your established churches doom me, and all that are out of their pale, as discarding some particular articles of your faith, to *perish everlastingly*, notwithstanding every thing that we may believe, or do. But I know that the candid and liberal of all persuasions are provided with some salvo for the conscientious heretic. But whatever may be your opinion with respect to me, which I know will be as favourable as you can make it, I have no doubt but, if I ever do get to heaven, I shall meet with both of you there. In that state our minds will be so much enlightened, that the bigotry which has contributed so much to the miseries of this life, but which has, at the same time, been a valuable exercise of christian candour, will no longer exist. With respect to myself, the time in which every thing of this kind will be cleared up, and no doubt to universal satisfaction, cannot be very distant; and the difference between my opinion, that it will be after an interval of rest in the grave, and yours that it will take place with respect to each individual immediately after his death, cannot be thought of much moment, by those who believe they shall live for ever after it.

With the highest esteem for your personal characters, though you are probably unknown to each other.

I am Gentlemen,

Your brother in the faith,

and hope of the Gospel.

J. PRIESTLEY.

Northumberland 1804.

PREFACE.

WHEN I wrote the Pamphlet entitled *Socrates and Jesus Compared*, which I was led to do from the perusal of Xenophon's Memorabilia, in order to form a more distinct idea than I then retained of the subjects and the manner of the teaching of Socrates, and from seeing his character in a different light from that in which it had been usually represented, I had no thoughts of doing any thing more in the same way. But my friends in general approving of the pamphlet, and seeing in the same light with myself the great superiority which it exhibited of the character and teaching of Jesus to that of this most moral, and most celebrated, of all the Grecian philosophers, I was urged to give a similar view of all the Grecian moralists, comparing their principles with those of revelation in general.

At first this appeared to me too great an undertaking at my age, and with increasing infirmities. But finding that my library, notwithstanding the destruction of a great part of it at the riots in Birmingham, was so far restored as to contain almost every book that I wanted for the purpose, having a predilection for the work, and abundant leisure in my present retired situation, I reperused the writings of all the Grecian moralists that have come to us, making all the extracts that I thought necessary, and then composed the different parts of the work with which I now present the reader; it was however not done in the order in which they are now arranged, but as they appeared to me of the most importance, giving directions to my son, that if I died before the work was compleated, he would publish what I had finished; having taken the precaution to transcribe, and prepare for the press, each of the separate parts before I undertook any other. In this manner, with much more ease, and I will add, more to my satisfaction, than I expected, I compleated my design.

My labour was the shorter, as I had nothing to do with the logic, the metaphysics, or the physics, of the writers all equally trifling and absurd, but only with such passages in their writings as related to the being, the attributes, and the providence of God, their sentiments concerning the human soul, and especially its destination after death, and their general

general principles of morals. For with these subjects only could they be brought into comparison with the doctrines of the scriptures. Also, my comparison extended no farther than till christianity became the religion of the Roman Emperors. For after this the tenets of the philosophers and those of the christians were strangely mixed, so that it might be said they borrowed from each other. I have therefore confined myself to the period in which they were entirely separate. For though after the promulgation of christianity the heathen philosophers had sufficient opportunity of acquainting themselves with its principles, they appear to have been entirely ignorant of them, or to have given little attention to them. This appears to me to have been the case with Marcus Antoninus, and others who lived long enough after the time of Christ. If they had any knowledge of christian principles, their bias was rather against than in favour of them.

There are several subdivisions of the Grecian philosophers which I have not noticed, but they were such as made only some small variation in some of the general systems of which I have given a particular account. The most considerable of them were Sceptics, and the Academics; but they advanced nothing new, and only doubted, and disputed, in different ways about the positions of others. For a more particular account of all the Grecian philosophers than it was to my purpose to give, I refer the reader to the excellent *History of Philosophy by Dr. Enfield*, most judiciously compiled from the elaborate work of Brucker. As the sentiments of the Grecian philosophers have been represented very differently, by writers who had different views in characterizing them, I thought it necessary to give numerous extracts from their own works; so that the reader may be confident that I have not made any mistake of importance in *my* account of them.

I once thought of adding another part, on the sentiments of Cicero, for though he was the founder of no sect, he was well acquainted with the principles of them all, and no doubt made his selection of those which he most approved. But besides that there is nothing of his own in any thing he has advanced on the several subjects, it is not easy to ascertain what his real sentiments were. His preference may in general be pretty well distinguished among the different speakers in his dialogues; but it was too great an object with him to embellish whatever he undertook to defend; so that

that there is often more of the orator, than of the philosopher, even in his philosophical works.

I can by no means persuade myself to think so highly of the religious sentiments of Cicero, and of their having been the real principles of his conduct, as Dr. Middleton does. He gives him every thing that is most essential in christianity, or what was by himself thought to be so; and among the rest a belief in the immortality of the soul, and its separate existence in a state of happiness or misery after death; whereas he expressly says there could hardly be found a foolish old woman who feared what had formerly been believed of the dreadful things in the shades below. De Natura deorum. (Lib. ii. cap. 2.) Yet on this subject, among others, Middleton says. *(Life of Cicero Vol. iii. p 240.)* "that Cicero has largely and "clearly declared his mind in many parts, of his "writings." Any person, however, may see in Dr. Middleton's work a large account of what is contained in the writings of Cicero on this subject; and to this elaborate, entertaining, and truly valuable work I refer the reader.

I have little doubt, but that the opinion expressed by Cæsar, in his speech, as given by Sallust, in the

the debate concerning the punishment of the Associates of Cataline, was that which was maintained by the senators in general, and all persons of rank and education at Rome; as it was not delivered by Cæsar as his own in particular, but evidently as what he apprehended would be that from which his hearers would not dissent. Cato, who spake after him, did not express any disapprobation of what he had said. Indeed as a stoic, he could not. Cicero himself was present, and did not contradict him. "In sorrow and distress," Cæsar said, "Death is a state of rest from all trouble, and not "of torment. It puts an end to all the evils to "which men are subject, and beyond it there is no "room for care or joy."

The result of the whole of this work, even to the most superficial observer, must be a sense of the infinite superiority of the doctrines of Revelation, and especially of those of christianity, to those of any heathen system whatever; and with this great advantage, that the principles of revelation are perfectly intelligible to the bulk of mankind, and the same with those which actually influence men in the common conduct of life; giving them a knowledge of what they have to hope from the practice of virtue, and what they have to fear in

conse-

consequence of vice. Moreover, these rules of life, coming immediately from the author of their being, have a great advantage in point of weight, and authority, far more than any mere reasoning, though ever so clear and satisfactory, could have given them.

Accordingly, the precepts of Moses were not, like the teachings of the Greek philosophers, confined to a few, but calculated for the use of the whole nation, the lowest as much as the highest among them. The doctrines and precepts of christianity are also equally intelligible to all mankind; and they are represented as of equal importance and concern to all, the slave as much as his master. Such a plan of general instruction was never practiced, nor, as far as appears, did the very idea of it ever occur to any of the Greek moralists. The lectures of the philosophers were given to select disciples, who generally paid for their instruction. With the common people they had nothing to do, while at the same time they encouraged them in their absurd and abominable religious rites, founded on that polytheism and idolatry which they themselves held in contempt; and this was founded on as groundless an opinion as any that was ever entertained by the lowest of the people,

ple, viz. that the welfare of the state depended upon the observance of them.

The attention I have given to this subject has increased the sense I had before of the great value of revelation to the virtue and happiness of mankind, and my gratitude to the universal parent, that I was born in a christian country, and in an age so much enlightened as the present. I rejoice also that I have been led, in the course of his providence, to do so much as I have done towards illustrating and defending the evidences of revelation, and towards purging it from those doctrines and practices which were discordant with it, and prevented its reception with many. I am willing to think that my *comparison of the institutions of the Hindoos, and other antient nations, with those of Moses*, and this work, which extends the comparison to all the sects of the Grecian philosophers, will eminently contribute to this end. Lastly, I am thankful to the author of my being that my life has been prolonged so far as to have been able to compleat my design. I could not have closed my life with more satisfaction than after a work of this kind. May the great Lord of the harvest send more, more zealous, and more able, labourers into his harvest.

CONTENTS.

CONTENTS.

CONTENTS.

On PLATONISM.

Of the PHILOSOPHY of ARISTOTLE.

Of the STOICAL PHILOSOPHY of MARCUS ANTONINUS and EPICTETUS.

CONTENTS.

Of the PHILOSOPHY of ARRIAN and SENECA.

Of the PHILOSOPHY of EPICURUS.

THE

PRINCIPLES OF THE GRECIAN PHILOSOPHY.

[PART I.]

ON

THE STATE OF RELIGIOUS AND MORAL PRINCIPLES IN GREECE BEFORE THE TIME OF PYTHAGORAS.

INTRODUCTION.

IN comparing the moral maxims of the heathen world with those of revelation, which is the object of this work, it is desirable to go as far back as we can, with any sufficient evidence, of what men really thought and did; and though with respect to Greece we cannot go so far back as we can with respect to Hindostan, and other oriental nations, we have two early writers on whom we may depend, viz. the poets HESIOD and HOMER; and they flourished, according to Newton, about eight hundred years before the christian æra:

We

We have also a poem of considerable length, containing precepts for the conduct of life, by THEOGNIS, which does not appear to have suffered by interpolation; and he flourished more than four hundred years before Christ; and also a shorter poem of PHOCYLIDES of the same age, thought by some to contain christian sentiments, and therefore to have been interpolated; we have also a collection of sayings of those who are generally called *the seven wise men of Greece*, who lived about six hundred years before Christ, preserved by Diogenes Laertius. Though all these are not of equal authority, I shall quote nothing from any of them but what will appear, by a comparison with others the antiquity of which is unquestionable, to be sufficiently to my purpose.

It is something remarkable that, near as Greece is to Palestine and Egypt, not only all *science*, properly so called, but a knowledge of the common and most useful *arts*, seems to have been unknown for ages in that country, till they were brought to them by the Phenicians or Egyptians, who came among them to find settlements, after flying from their own countries, and who found them in a state of the greatest barbarism, and divided into a great

number

number of *clans*; for *nations* or *states* they did not deserve to be called; and in a state of hostility with each other, as mankind in a similar situation are always found to be.

These wandering tribes of Greece, similar to those in North America at present (for they were a long time in no better, but rather in a worse state with respect to civilization,) must no doubt, have had some notions of religion; since no people in the world have been intirely without them; but what they were in that rude state of the country it is impossible to trace. The sacred rites and modes of worship that we find accounts of in their writers were acknowledged to have been borrowed from Egypt, and other countries. And even *this* was in so early a period, before they had any writers, that the observance of them had been from time immemorial; so that the veneration they had acquired from their antiquity was not to be shaken.

Whatever they were, and they were different in every part of the country, and more or less in every different town and hamlet, they were supposed to be connected with the well-being of the place; so that it would have been thought hazardous to make any change in them. Nor do we find that this was ever done in any heathen country. They might adopt new gods, and new modes of worship, but they never abandoned their own antient ones.

This partial civilization of Greece must have been a considerable time after the greatest part of the knowledge derived from revelation had been lost in the East, as will be evident to any person who compares what he finds on this subject in the earliest of the Greek writers with the book of Job, to say nothing of the writings of Moses. Job and his friends, though probably not themselves favoured with any revelation, appear to have had a clear knowledge of the being, and the righteous government of the one true God, the maker of the world, and of all things in it, and also of a future state of righteous retribution. At least so it clearly appears to me, though of late, and only of late, some christian writers have questioned this. But how miserably bewildered were the wisest of the Greeks with respect to these subjects. Of the knowledge of a future state, on the only principle of reason, as well as revelation, viz. that of a proper *resurrection*, we do not perceive the least trace among them. Instead of this, they had adopted a notion of a *separate soul*, or a *ghost*, descending after death into a

region

region below the surface of the earth, and the most absurd fables relating to their condition there; though these, do not appear to have had any credit with the writers, nor probably with any persons of much thought and reflection among them.

Section I.

Of the Obligation to the Worship of the Gods in general.

The general and established opinion of a superior power, or powers, governing the affairs of the world and of men, and the obligation that men were under to worship them, according to the customary rites of each people, was universal. And this was not only the persuasion of the vulgar, but of all the writers without any exception. In a later period it is probable enough that what several of the writers advance on this subject might arise from a wish not to shock the prejudices of the populace, but with respect to the period of which I am now treating, there seems to be no reason to doubt of their sincerity; the precepts on this subject are so numerous, and urged in so emphatical a manner by them all. The obligation to worship the gods is urged by Solon, one of whose sayings was, "honour the gods, rever- ence thy parents."

None of the seven wise men of Greece, can be said to have been writers, and therefore we have not sufficient authority for their real opinions. But Theognis and Phocylides were; and in the poem of the former, we find (v. 170.) "Pray to the gods "who have great power, for without the gods men "have neither good nor evil." Here we see the belief of this writer in the providence, as well as in the existence, of the gods; but we shall have more abundant evidence of this hereafter. Phocylides says (v. 7.) "In the first place worship the gods, "then honour thy parents, judge no man unjustly, "for afterwards God will judge thee." Indeed, what this poet says of *God* may with some reason be suspected to have been drawn from the principles of revelation, and therefore to be an interpolation. For he says, v. 48, "There is one God, wise, pow- "erful, and self sufficient."

Hesiod, though in his *Theogony* he retails all the Grecian fables concerning the origin and de- scent of the gods, all of whom he derives from the *earth*, which was therefore prior to them all, yet his poem intitled *On Works* contains excellent senti- ments

ments, and good advice on this subject, as well as on many others. Addressing his brother, he says, (Lib. I. v 334.) "According to thy ability, sacri- "fice to the immortal gods morning and evening, "that they may shew thee favour, and that thou may- "est purchase the possesions of others, and others "not purchase thine. Pray (Lib. II. v. 84.) to Ju- "piter and Ceres, that you may have a good in- "crease." According to Hesiod Jupiter destroy- ed a whole race of men, because they did not give due honour to the gods, (Lib. I. v. 138.)

Many of Hesiod's precepts relating to religion, and the business of husbandry too, savour of a ridi- culous superstition; but at this we cannot wonder, considering in how early and ignorant an age he lived. "Do not," says he (Lib. II. v. 343.) "make libation, to Jupiter with unwashen hands, "nor to the other immortal gods; for they will not "hear, but abominate, such prayers." His poem *On Days* contains hardly any thing besides directi- ons of the most superstitious and absurd kind, but his two books *On Works* contain many excellent precepts, both of morality, and common pru- dence.

SECTION II.

Of the Superiority of Jupiter, the principal God of the Greeks.

Notwithstanding the polytheism of the Greeks, they retained so much of the primitive doctrine of *one supreme God*, that they gave this pre-eminence to their Jupiter; and indeed seem to have ascribed to him universal dominion, and every attribute requisite for the exercise of it. We see this even in Homer, notwithstanding his account of such actions of the same Jupiter as sink him far below the level of many men. But a strolling bard, who got his living by accommodating himself to all kinds of people, could not contradict the popular tales of his countrymen, absurd as he might think them; and they served, as a very convenient *machinery*, as it is now called, for his poem.

Besides that one of the epithets of Jupiter in Homer (μητιέτα) implies wisdom, he is expressly said, (Iliad, Lib. XIII. v. 631.) to "excel all the gods "and men in wisdom"; and when the wisdom of Ulysses and also that of Hector, is praised, it is compar-

compared to that of Jupiter (Iliad. Lib. II. 168. Lib. VII. v. 74) He is also stiled *the omnipotent* (Iliad. Lib. II. v. 115.) and said "to command mortals "and immortals" (Lib. XII. v. 242.) He is represented as asserting his own superiority to all the gods and goddesses, both in wisdom and power, and they all allow it (Iliad, Lib. VIII. v 9) &c. When the demolition of several cities, particularly named, is ascribed to him, it is added, "whose power is the "greatest." (Iliad, Lib. IX. v. 25.)

Theognis had the same idea of the great superiority of Jupiter, when he says (v 802.) "not even "Jupiter, who rules over mortals and immortals, "can please all men."

With respect to the issue of the Trojan war, Homer says, "the will of Jupiter was done." (Iliad, Lib. I. v 5.) as if the whole had depended upon him; and yet there remains some doubt whether there was not, even in the opinion of Homer himself, another power in some respects superior to him, and which he could not control, viz. *Fate* as we shall see hereafter.

We could not expect such attributes as these of the greatest wisdom and power in the son of Saturn, though called *the father of gods and men* (Iliad,

Lib. XV. v. 47.) for according to Hesiod, this Saturn was only the youngest son, or production, of the earth and the heavens, and had no higher epithet than that of crafty (αγκυλομητης) and the *heavens*, one of his parents, was the offspring of the *earth*, the other of them.

This universal opinion of the great superiority of Jupiter had certainly a higher origin than Hesiod's Theogony gives him, and must have been the remains of a much purer system of theology, which taught the doctrine of *one God*, infinitely wise, powerful, and good, a favourer of virtue, and superintending all the affairs of men, as we shall see this Jupiter to do.

SECTION III.

Of Providence.

The farther we proceed in this examination, the more convinced we shall be that the Jupiter of the more sensible of the Greeks was a very different person from the son of the crafty Saturn, or the lecherous deity of the vulgar, and of the stage; and we shall see that they gave him a field of exertion suitable to the extraordinary powers with which they

they invested him. According to them, he was nothing less than the supreme Governor of the world, and the sovereign disposer of all things in it, and not only of such things as cannot be fore-seen or prevented by man, but of such as seem to depend upon human exertion.

Wealth is, to appearance, most certainly acquired by industry and economy, directed by good sense in the conduct of men's affairs; but notwithstanding this, it is constantly represented by these writers as the gift of Jupiter, and if a man be poor, it is by them ascribed to his not favouring him. Hesiod says (On Works, Lib. I. v. 5.) "It is Ju-" piter who raises up one, and depresses another. "It is Jupiter who gives poverty to men," (On Works, Lib. II. v. 257.) Theognis says (v. 157. 165.) "No person is rich or poor," and he adds, "good or bad," without a deity. He makes "some "rich, and others poor. God surrounds a good "man with every blessing, good success, and free-" dom from folly; and we ought to bear whatever "the gods impose upon us." (v. 591.) Agreeably to this he prays (v. 1115.) "May Apollo and "Jupiter grant that I may live free from evil, en-" joying health and riches." He says, however

(v. 863.

(v. 863.) "God gives wealth to many worthless "men, who are of no use to themselves, or their "friends;" Still, however it is disposed of, it is the gift of the gods. And he says (v. 325.) "If "the gods give a bad man wealth and riches, like a "fool, he cannot restrain his malice, but a just man "is the same in good or bad fortune." He therefore reasonably makes this a motive to a good use of riches. "Whatever God gives to you, of that "give to the poor." He also makes it a motive to bear misfortunes with patience. "In misfortune "pray to the gods, and make no boast. (v. 357.)

According to the poetical representation of Homer (Iliad. Lib. XXIV. v. 527) "There are placed "at the gates of Jupiter two casks, one of them "containing good, and the other evil," out of which it is hereby intimated that he gives to man out of one or other of them as he pleases. According to the uniform language of Homer, *honour* is also the gift of Jupiter, as well as advantages of every other kind. (Iliad. Lib. II. v. 198.)

The events of *war* are, according to Homer, no less at the disposal of Jupiter, than wealth and honor, though the Greeks had a god, Mars, whose peculiar province it was to attend to it. He is expressly

pressly called (Iliad. Lib. IV. v 84.) "the arbiter "of war" and is said, (Iliad. Lib. II. v. 309.) "to "give the victory to whom he pleases It is he" he says "(Iliad. Lib. II. v. 94.) that makes a man "a warrior, and he soon turns to flight the valiant" (Iliad, Lib. XVI. v. 690.) He even inspired Ajax with fear (Lib. XI. v. 543.) Hesiod, agreeably to these sentiments, says (On Works, Lib. I. v. 225.) "Jupiter does not visit a just nation with war."

In like manner this poet considers the same Jupiter as the giver of *wine*, though Bacchus is said to have discovered it, to have imparted it to men, and to preside over every thing relating to it. Nay, Hesiod, in three or four different places of his Theogny, gives the gods in general the glorious title of (δοτηρες εαων,) *the givers of good.* (v. 46, 633, 664, &c.) It was a saying of Bias, "Whatever good you do "ascribe it to the gods." These are precious remains of a very remote antiquity, derived no doubt, from the most genuine and purest source.

In order to this government of the world, and the sovereign distributions of every thing in it, it was necessary that the gods, and especially Jupiter, the chief of them, should know every thing that passes in it; and accordingly this is taken for granted

granted by all the writers within this period. "Do "not" says Theognis, (v. 1195.) "swear falsely "by the gods. This is not to be borne, for no-"thing can be concealed from them." "The "eye of Jupiter," says Hesiod, (On Works, Lib. I. v. 265.) "who sees every thing, and under-"stands every thing, is not ignorant of any thing "that passes within a state." He is therefore frequently appealed to in Homer as always present, and a witness to contracts, as in (Iliad, Lib. VII. v. 76. 411.) He is prayed to (Iliad, Lib. VII. v. 178.) to determine the lot that was to decide which of the Grecian warriors was to fight Hector. It was a saying of Thales (who said that God had no beginning and will have no end,) that "neither "the actions, nor the thoughts, of bad men are con-"cealed from the gods."

As attending more especially to the affairs of states, and kingdoms, Jupiter is represented as "the guardian of kings," (Iliad. Lib. II. v. 97.) and the Greeks are said to have derived their laws from him (Lib. I. v. 239.) How uncertain any particular event may be with respect to man, it is not so, according to Theognis, with respect to God. "It is difficult," he says (v. 1074.) "to "know

" know how a thing that is not finished will end, " or how God will bring it about."

This is frequently the language of our scriptures with respect to the constant attention that God gives to the affairs of men, distributing health, wealth, power, success in war, and every other natural advantage, or withholding them, and appointing in their place calamity of every kind, as he pleases, and for reasons that it is not in the power of man to comprehend. These heathens do not, however, seem to have entertained the same persuasion that the sacred writers had, of the wisdom and goodness of the Supreme Being in these mysterious dispensations, which, whether they could distinguish or not, they always take for granted. These heathens also never express the noble sentiment that occurs so frequently in the scriptures, that hardships of every kind are frequently appointed to be the lot of the righteous, for an exercise of their virtue, and as the correction of a kind and judicious parent; and that a proper reception of them, and behaviour under them, will entitle the virtuous sufferers to a glorious reward. Having no knowledge of a future state, they could not see so far into the conduct of providence.

SECTION

SECTION IV.

Of Jupiter's Regard to Virtue.

As the early Greek writers have given to Jupiter the government of the world, though not the creation of it, and invested him with powers equal to it, they have not failed to give him a disposition worthy of that high station, representing him as the friend of virtue in general, and especially of justice, becoming so great a governor.

Hesiod has many excellent observations, expressed with great energy, on this subject. " Let us" he says (On Works, Lib. I. v.35.) " give right judg-
" ments in contests, for these are from Jupiter. Ex-
" ercise justice, and forget violence, this is the law
" that Jupiter imposes upon men, and that only
" beasts of prey should live by violence and slaugh-
" ter, (On Works, Lib. I. v.275.) Jupiter, see-
" ing at a distance, punishes injustice and wicked-
,, ness, (On Works, Lib. I v. 236.) the people die,
" women do not bear children, families decrease,
" and their ships perish. To just men Jupiter
" gives wealth, and his descendants prosper, but the
" un-

"unjust man injures himself, and his posterity." (On Works, Lib. I. v. 280.)

To enforce these admonitions, he gives the following beautiful allegory, "O kings, respect justice; for the gods, who are conversant among men, see all the unjust judgments of those who do not regard their threatenings. For there are three myriads, the sons of Jupiter on the earth, the guardians of men, who take an account both of justice and injustice, having vestments of air, and visiting all parts of the earth. Justice is a virgin, the daughter of Jupiter; and if any person offend her, she immediately complains of it to Jupiter, and the people suffer for the offences of their kings, who do not decide justly." (On Works, Lib. I. v. 246.) Lastly, he represents Jupiter as having resolved to destroy the fifth, and last. race of men, on account of their vices and depravity in general. (On Works, Lib. I. v. 178.)

Theognis concurs in the same sentiments with Hesiod in representing Jupiter as the friend and benefactor of good men. "The wealth," (v. 197.) "he says that Jupiter gives to a just man is permanent. By injustice and oppresssion many acquire wealth; but it will be lost, for the mind of God is superior."

More especially, Jupiter, and the gods in general, are represented as offended at *perjury*, and determined to punish it. "The immortal gods," says Phocylides (v. 15.) "hate a false oath, whoever takes it." And Theognis says, "never "swear that any thing shall not be; for the gods "are angry at it." (v. 659.) In Homer Jupiter is frequently appealed to for the observance of oaths, and requested to punish the guilty, (Iliad, Lib. III. v. 321.) Talthybias calls to witness in the first place Jupiter, stiled on this occasion, by the remarkable character of *the greatest and the best*, then the sun, the earth, and the furies, who he says punish the perjured under the earth, (Iliad, Lib. XIX. v. 257.)

Other vices are occasionally mentioned as incurring the indignation of Jupiter. "Father Jupiter "will not favour a liar" (Iliad, Lib. IV. v. 235.) "May the celestial gods," says Theognis (v. 850.) "destroy the man that shall by smooth speeches "deceive his friend." Hesiod says (On Works, Lib. I. v. 329.) "He who deceives the orphan, or "abuses his aged parents, Jupiter is certainly angry "with him, and at the last he will give an account "of all his unjust actions." In Homer Menelaus ians prays that "Jupiter may give him to punish "the wicked Alexander, that hereafter all men may "dread to injure a person who has received them "with kindness." (Iliad. Lib. III. v. 11.) Chilon being asked what Jupiter was doing, said, "He is humbling the proud and exalting the hum-"ble."

No Jew or Christian could appeal with more confidence to the justice and equity of the true God than these persons do to their Jupiter. It is evident, therefore, that, whatever name they gave this object of their worship they had the same idea of his general character; and this must have been derived from the same source. The belief of a righteous governor of the world appears never to have been wholly abandoned by mankind. Though the name was changed, and multiplicity took the place of unity, what was most essential to the righteous administration of affairs was, in a considerable degree, though accompanied with much superstition, retained. The heathens were deficient chiefly in their ignorance of a future state, in which the seeming irregularities, and many unaccountable appearances in this life, will be rectified to universal satisfaction.

Section V.

Of the Influence of the Fates.

It is something remarkable that, notwithstanding the omnipotence which the heathens ascribed to their gods, and their control over the affairs of men, they had an idea of a power which the gods themselves either could not, or did not chuse to oppose. This was *Fate*, or *the Fates*. And yet this was a divinity to which they never ascribed any degree of wisdom.

According to Hesiod, the Fates were the daughters of Jupiter, and he gave them this extraordinary power. "Jupiter" (and whom on this occasion he styles "*the wise*, μητιετα) produced the Parcœ "(μοιρας) Clotho, Lachesis, and Atropos, to whom "he gave the greatest honour, who distribute good "and evil to mortal men," Theogonia v. 905. But in another place of the same poem (v. 211) he says that, "Night produced odious Fate (μορον) "and the black Parcœ and Death, without the "concurrence of any deity—— and the fatal god-"desses, and cruel Parcœ, Clotho, Lachesis, "and

" and Atropos, who appoint good and evil to men " that are born, who revenging the offences of men " and gods, never remit of their anger till they have punished the offender." Here the same powers have a different origin, and are altogether independent of Jupiter, or any of the gods, and superior to them all.

Besides the sovereign power over life and death, and external advantages of every kind, the affections and characters of men are sometimes ascribed to these fates. " The Fates," says Homer, (Iliad, Lib. XXIV. v. 49.) " give a patient mind to man." However, with respect to the important article of life or death, their decision was never violated; and the time, and all the circumstances, of a man's death were determined by them, as well as the death itself. Thus Neptune assures Achilles, who knew that he was never to return from the siege of Troy, that is was not his fate to be drowned in the river, when he apprehended that he was in great danger from it. (Iliad, Lib. XXI. v. 291.) He wishes that he might die by the hand of Hector, a brave man, but he knew that he should fall by a less noble hand. (Iliad, Lib. XXI. v. 278.)

Whatever the gods might wish, they never failed to acquiesce in the known decision of the fates. Achilles, lamenting his destiny, says that "Hercu-"les, though most dear to Jupiter, was conquered "by Fate, and the anger of Juno (Iliad, Lib. XVIII. v. 118.) "It was in the fates," he says, (Iliad. Lib. XVIII. v. 328.) "that two friends of "his should die before Troy, as well as that he "was not to return to Greece." It was one of the sayings of Pittacus. "The Gods cannot op-"pose Fate."

On several occasions the gods express some degree of fear least the orders of the fates should be violated. Neptune, expressing his regard for Æneas, advises him not to fight before the death of Achilles (Iliad, Lib. XX. v. 336.) though he knew that it was not in the fates that he should die by his hand. Both Apollo and Jupiter express their concern lest the Greeks should take Troy before the time ordained by the fates. (Iliad, Lib. XXI. v. 516. XX. v. 30.)

On some occasions Jupiter, who is said to have given this great power to the fates, seems to think it was in his power to control them, and to have been half inclined to do it; but he yielded to the remonstrances of the other gods, who opposed his

his resolution. When Hector was driven by Achilles round the walls of Troy, Jupiter expressed an inclination to save him from death. But Minerva says to him, (Iliad, Lib. XXII. v. 180.) "Would you deliver from death a mortal man, "destined to die by the fates? Do what you "please, but we, the rest of the gods, will not give "our consent." He acknowledged that it was in the fates that Sarpedon should die by the hand of Patroclus, and wished to convey him to a place of safety; but Juno expostulating with him on the subject, he acquiesced. (Iliad. Lib. XVI. v. 432.) The independence of the decision of these fates on the will of the gods seems not to have been a fixed principle. For Ulysses, speaking to Tiresias in the Elysian fields says, according to Homer, (Odyssey, Lib. XI. v. 139.) "Perhaps the gods them-"selves have decreed these things. (επεκλωσαν) At what time this decision of the fates was made, is not said in these writers; but it was commonly supposed to be at the birth of every particular person. It was, however, considered as so irrevocable, that these fates, though goddesses, were never prayed to, it being taken for granted that whatever they had advanced it would never be altered.

There was another celestial power acknowledged by the Greeks, but seemingly not so early as the times of Hesiod and Homer, as they make no mention of her. This was *Fortune*. For whatever was afterwards ascribed to her, is by him, and all the other writers that I have quoted, ascribed to Jupiter, or some other of the gods.

Neither of these powers are, however, known in the scriptures. According to them, every thing in the world, life and death, riches and poverty, success, or the want of it, in war, and undertakings of any other kind, are ascribed to the providence of that *one God*, who created and governs all things, and whose will, independently of any such powers as those of Fate or Fortune, decides upon every thing. To him we are taught to look for every thing, as being wholly dependant upon him, and accountable to him. This frees the mind from that perplexity, to which the wisest of the heathens must have been subject, while they had any apprehension of this *blind fate* to which, whether willingly or unwillingly, their gods themselves, without excepting even Jupiter, submitted.

SECTI-

SECTION VI.

Of Moral Duties, and also of Death and the Consequences of it.

Almost all the writers that I have quoted in this part of my work deliver excellent precepts both respecting *morals* properly so called, and the prudent conduct of life, similar to the *Proverbs of Solomon*, to which they will often well bear to be compared. Many parts of Hesiods poem *On Works*, and the sentences of Theognis, are particularly valuable on this account, though the superstition of the former, or rather that of the age and the country in which he lived, as appears in the second part of the poem viz. *On Days*, is extreme.

On the subject of *death*, and its consequences, there is a remarkable silence in all the serious writers of this period. The knowledge of the doctrine of a resurrection was completely lost, but there are traces of a belief that the soul survives the grave, though not of any state of righteous retribution, in which the righteous will be rewarded, and the wicked punished for their actions here, except in those fables of Homer concerning the state of ghosts in tartarus and elysium, probably not seriously believed by himself; so that the great sanction of virtue, familiar to Jews and Christians was unknown to them.

In Phocylides are some sentences which express a clear belief of souls surviving the grave. " Im-" mortal souls," he says (v. 110.) " free from old " age, live for ever. All the dead are equal," (v. 105.) " but God governs souls. We hope to " see the remains of the dead come out of the earth " into light, after which they will be gods. For " incorruptible Souls remain in the dead. The " spirit is the image of God given to mortals," (v. 100.) According to this the soul continues attached to the body some time after it is dead, which was the opinion of the Egyptians, and the cause, as it is thought of their endeavouring to preserve the bodies so long by embalming them, and keeping them in their houses.

After the perusal of this, how happy ought we to think ourselves for enjoying the glorious light of the Gospel, by which, and by which alone, *life and immortality are brought to light*. Without this light, *the wisdom of the world* availed but little to the moral improvement and happiness of man. And as we proceed we shall find no increase of light, but rather of darkness, with respect to this subject.

OF

THE PHILOSOPHY

of

PYTHAGORAS.

INTRODUCTION.

PYTHAGORAS appears to have been the first of all the Greeks who gave his whole time to philosophy either in the acquisition of knowledge or in the communication of it to others. He is said to have been a native of Samos, and after having had some instruction from Pherecydes of Scyros, (of whom little is known, except that he had some knowledge of Oriental philosophy,) he went to Egypt; where, having the patronage of the king Amasis, he obtained leave to be initiated into the religion and philosophy of the Egyptians. The priests made him undergo a very severe discipline, including circumcision, but he submitted to every thing they enjoined; and, continuing in the country twenty two years, may be presumed to have acquired all the

know-

knowledge that could be obtained there. Finding on his return no sufficient encouragement, in his endeavours to open a school of philosophy in his own country, he finally settled at Crotona, in that part of Italy which, in consequence of having been colonized by Greeks, was called Magna Græcia; from which his sect of philosophy was called the *Italic*. Here his disciples were very numerous, and they continued with more or less reputation about two hundred years.

It is not possible to ascertain with any certainty what it was that was taught by Pythagoras himself. For, besides committing nothing to writing, he enjoined the strictest secrecy on all his pupils, training them to the most severe discipline, the first part of which is said to have been an uninterrupted silence of five years. By this means nothing of his doctrines transpired till a little before the time of Plato, which was something more than a century after the establishment of the sect, when several philosophers in Greece having acquired much reputation by their writings, the masters of the Italic schools began to publish what they had been taught of its doctrines, but mixed with their own.

Of these later Pythagoreans there are extant two curious and valuable treatises, one by Ocellus

Luca-

Lucanus and the other by Timœus Locrus, besides many large extracts by Stobœus from the writings of Archytas, and besides many fragments from Theages, the Sentences of Democrates, Secundus, Demophilus and Sextus, and verses which have obtained for their excellence the title of *golden*, written as Fabricius supposes by Empedocles, but certainly by some learned Pythagorean. From these sources we must now be content to collect the best account that we can of the general principles of the Pythagorean philosophy. They are all published in *Gale's Opuscula Mythologica*, and some of the latter of them I suspect to contain sentiments that do not properly belong to any system of heathen philosophy, but to have been borrowed from Christianity. In the choice of these I have been very sparing, and they will be noticed, as it is my object not to go beyond the time when Christianity became the religion of the Roman emperors.

From the genuine tracts above-mentioned it will not be difficult to collect a pretty just idea of the principles of this sect, at least as improved by the followers of Pythagoras; and as to what he taught that has never come to light, which was probably something more near to the oriental philosophy, it is of little consequence to know at present.

SECTI-

Section I.

Concerning God.

That God is the maker and governor of the world, and the sovereign disposer of all events, was taken for granted by all the Pythagoreans, and there is a great display of genuine piety in what remains of their writings. Timœus says "God is "the author and parent of all things, but what is "produced by him we see with our eyes." The honour due to God, and to other objects of worship according to their respective ranks, is inculcated in the first of the golden verses of Pythagoras. "In the first place honor the gods, as the "laws direct, and observe oaths. Then venerate "the famous heroes, and the infernal gods, perform-"ing with respect to them the rites directed by "the laws. Then honour thy parents, and nearest "relations." This probably refers to some religious ceremony in honour of men's ancestors, which is to this day a great article in the religion of the Hindoos.

All this, however, might be in obedience to the laws, the omission of which would have been punish-

punishable; but the author of these verses farther directs to begin no work without asking the divine blessing for its success. Evil, as well as good, is here ascribed to the providence of God. "Whatever portion you have of the calamity that "befals men through the divine appointment bear "with patience, and without complaining. How-"ever, remedy the evil if you can, and consider "that the Parcœ do not assign much of this to good men." Here the assignment of the Parcœ are considered as the same with the will of the gods. One of the sayings collected by Demophilus is, "God sends evil to men not in anger, for an-"ger is foreign to God. This takes place when "things come by accident, whereas nothing can "come to God but what he wills."

There is much good sense, as well as piety, in the precepts of Pythagoras relating to God, at least such as are ascribed to him by those who collected his sayings. Among them are the following. "Gifts and sacrifices confer no honour "on God, but a pious mind joins it finally to "God. For things that are similar must be joined "to things similar, (Dem.) God has not on the "earth a place more suitable to him than a chaste

"and

" and pure mind. (Ib.) If you consider that " whatever is done by the mind or the body is " seen by God; you will revere his presence, from " whom nothing can be concealed; for you will " have God residing in your breast," (Ib.) Having mentioned a variety of good works, the golden verses add, " These will put you in the way of di- " vine virtue."

It is the more probable that these pious sentiments were the genuine produce of the Pythagorean school, as it was nearer to the patriarchal times, and something like those in the book of Job, when true piety was still more prevalent, and more free from superstition. We shall, however, observe a lamentable departure from the simple idea of revelation, when we see what the Pythagoreans say concerning the structure of the world, and the nature of the human soul, on which subjects they led the way to all the wild ideas of Plato and some of the sentiments of Aristotle, though these do not seem to have been willing to acknowledge their obligations to them.

SECTION

Section II.

Of the Structure of the World.

We shall see in this section how far the minds of the most intelligent men can wander from reason and common sense, when they speculate on subjects that are above their comprehension, and on which, having no light from revelation, it was impossible that they should get any at all.

Moses with great simplicity, as expressing all that he believed, and all that he could know, on the subject, says "In the beginning God created the heavens and the earth. But these philosophers, having lost every tradition of this kind, (which, however, was retained in the East) maintained that the universe had no beginning, as well as that it will have no end. "All plants and animals, says Ocel-"lus Lucanus (Cap. 1. & 3.) and also the human "race, have always been, and will ever be as they "now are." This, too, is contrary to the doctrine of our scriptures, which holds out to us a far more pleasing prospect, viz. a perpetual progress to a better state of things, and the great advantage which

which virtuous men will derive from it, in their own constant improvement, and the removal of every impediment to it, with every thing else that is painful and distressing to them. Of this no heathen philosopher had the least idea.

Notwithstanding the opinion of the Pythagoreans, of one Supreme God, they admitted many inferior deities, and particularly considered *the world* as endued with life and divinity, and in their account of the formation of it we shall see the *intelligible ideas* of Plato, which he, no doubt, borrowed from them. "God," says Timæus, "formed the world out of all kinds of matter. It is "one, the only begotten, endued with a soul and "reason. When God willed to produce a per"fect offspring, he made this generated god, not to "be perishable from any cause except by the god "that made it. The world therefore remains as it "was created by God, free from corruption and "death. It is the best of all created things, since "it arose from the best of causes. In this the cre"ator proposed to himself no model made by hand, "but his own *ideas*, and *intelligible essence*, according to which, when things are made with exquisite art, they are the most beautiful, and require not to be mended by any new operation."

In a farther account of these *ideas*, he says, "There is in the universe something that is per-"manent, and intelligible, the examplar of the "things that are produced, which are in a perpetu-"al flux. They are called *ideas*, and are comprehended by the mind." He afterwards calls these ideas *forms* which are comprehended by the mind, and *science*. "Before the heavens existed, there "were *forms*, and *matter*, and God, who is good, "and is the author of that which is best."

The Pythagoreans speak of every thing as adapted to *harmonical numbers*, and on this subject Timœus goes into many particulars, which it would be tedious to recite. "Of these," however, he says "the soul of the world is constituted. Life," he says, "supports the body, and the cause of this is "the soul (ψυχα). Harmony supports the world, "and the cause (αἴτιος) of this is God." Fragmenta.

"God," he says, "placed the soul of the world "in its center, and also produced it externally," probably meaning that, though seated in the center, its operation goes beyond it.

The world is not the only inferior deity in this system. "In every part of the world," says Ocellus

lus Lucanus (cap. 3.) "there are inhabitants of a nature proper to it, as gods in the heavens, men upon the earth, in the higher regions demons, and of course the race of man must always continue.

Matter these philosophers seem to have considered as having always existed, independently of the deity, and as having been subject to laws which he could not wholly control. "Whence," Timœus says, though with some degree of obscurity. "There are two causes of all things, *mind* of those "things which are produced with reason, and *ne-* "*cessity* of those which exist by a kind of force, "according to the powers and properties of body." They, therefore, did not want any other cause of evil besides matter.

Section III.

Of the Human Soul.

According to these Pythagoreans, the human soul is not of a nature so distinct from the body, but that it has both some connection with it, and some properties in common with it. "The source of "vice," says Timœus, is in pleasure and grief,

 "desire

"desire and fear, which being excited in the bo-"dy, get mixed with the soul, and have obtained "various names from their various effects, as love, "desire," &c. so that the *passions* are common to the soul and the body, though they are first excited in the latter.

They maintained, however, the superiority of the mind to the body as when Archytas (Gale's, Op. myth. p. 732.) says, "In all human things wis-"dom is most excellent, as the sight is more so "than the other senses, the mind (νους) than the soul "(ψυχα) and the sun than the stars." Here we have two parts of the soul, or of the man, distinguished by their respective names, the former, signifying the seat of intelligence, and the other that of mere animal life.

Timœus explains this division of the soul farther when he says, "One part of the human soul is "endued with reason and intelligence, but the o-"ther is without reason, and stupid. The former "is the more excellent, but both have their seat a-"bout the head, that the other parts of the soul, "and of the body too, might be subservient to it, "as being under the same tabernacle of the body. "But that part of the soul which is without reason,

and

"and which is prone to anger, has its seat about "the heart; and that which has concupiscence "has its seat about the liver. But the brain is the "principle, and root, of the spinal marrow; and "in it the soul has the seat of its government.,' (Gale's, opus. myth. p. 556. 557.)

Theages divides the soul in the same manner. "One of the parts," he says, "has reason, another "anger, and the third desire. The virtue of pru-"dence," he says, "belongs to the first part, for-"titude to the second, and temperance to the third, "and justice is the virtue of the whole soul," (Ibid. p. 688.)

How much more simple and satisfactory is the short account that Moses gives of the formation and constituent principles of man. After giving an account of the formation of all other animals, he says that in the last place, God made man *of the dust of the ground*, and then breathed into him the breath of life, after which he was a living soul, or being; that is, after *the man* was completely made, with all his powers, those of the mind, as well as those of the body, God enabled him to *breath*, by which all his powers were excited, and brought into actual exercise. Nothing is here said of any division of the principle of life, but he adds, that *man was made in the likeness of God*, meaning probably having capacity of knowing, and of having intercourse with him, which other animals have not; and that he *gave him dominion over all the other animals*, properties which he has, and fully exercises.

The account given by these Pythagoreans of the state of the soul after death, is still more unsatisfactory and inconsistent. According to the golden verses, the soul is immortal. "If," says the author (v. 70.) "when you have left the body, you arrive at the "free ether, you will be with the incorruptible "immortal gods, and be no longer mortal." Timæus gives the following more detailed account of the power of man to attain this state, as well as of the punishment of those whose vices disqualify them for it; but it is with a sufficient intimation, that he considered it as founded on mere fable, calculated for the use of the vulgar, and by no means agreeable to truth, so that it is probable that at this time the Pythagoreans had wholly abandoned all belief in a future state, "Music," he says, "and the "directrix of it philosophy, are adapted by God, "and the laws, for the improvement of the mind, "and they accustom, persuade, and compel, that part of the soul which has no reason to be gentle,

free

" free from anger, and desire........ Science, " and antient and venerable philosophy, free the " mind from false and vain opinions, and great ig- " norance, and raise it to the contemplation of hea- " venly things, in the knowledge of which, if a man " so conduct himself as to be content with his lot, " and with the accidents of life, and thus aspire af- " ter a moderate and temperate life, he is in the " way to true felicity. And certainly he to whom " God has given this lot is led by the truest opini- " ons to the most happy life. But if on the other " hand any be refractory, and will not obey these " sacred precepts, he will be amenable to those " laws which denounce both celestial and infernal " punishments. Unrelenting punishments await " the unhappy manes, and other things mentioned " by the Ionic poet, as derived from tradition, by " the hearing of which he wished to draw the minds " of men to religion and purity. On this account " I approve of his conduct. As we cure diseased " bodies by unwholesome medicines if they will not " yield to those that are wholesome, so we restrain " minds with deceitful discourses, if they will not " yield to true ones. On this account, too, fo- " reign punishments are denounced," (that is,

 such

such as were believed by foreign nations,) "as the "transmigrations of souls into various bodies, "viz. those of the idle into the bodies of women, "murderers into those of wild beasts, of the libidi-"nous into those of hogs or bears, of the light and "rash into fowls, of the idle and foolish into aqua-"tic animals" (Gale's, Op. Myth. p. 565. 566.) &c. Certainly the man who could write this could have no belief of any future punishment of the wicked, whatever he might think of the state of the virtuous after death.

But when the question *what is death* was put to Secundus, his answer is decisively against any future state at all. "It is," he says, "an eternal "sleep, the dread of the rich, the desire of the poor, "the inevitable event, the robber of man, the flight "of life, and the dissolution of all things." (Gale's, Op. Myth p. 641.)* Such were the comfortless prospects of this philosophy in its most advanced state. What a wretched choice would a christian make by exchanging his religion for this.

Section IV.

Of Good and Evil, Virtue and Vice.

The writings of the Pythagoreans contain numberless excellent moral maxims and precepts, expressed in the most forcible language, and their account of what is *good* is agreeable to common sense, which we shall see was not the case with many of the philosophers who came after them.

"Some goods," says Archytas, "are desired "on their own account, some on the account of o-"ther things, and a third both for their own sake, "and that of other things. What then is that "good which is desired on its own account, and "not for the sake of any thing else? It is happi-"ness. For the sake of this we desire every thing "else, but this for the sake of nothing farther. "(Gale's, Op. Myth. p. 674.) A good man is not "immediately and necessarily happy, but a happy "man must be good. You must not," says Demophilus, "hastily pronounce that man happy "who depends upon any thing that is liable to "change and decay, but on himself, and on God. "This only is firm and stable." (Ib. p. 624.)

There

There was a great degree of austerity in the discipline, and general maxims of the Pythagoreans, which forbade all unnecessary gratifications. With respect to the commerce of the sexes, Ocellus Lucanus, (Ch. 4. Gale's Op. Myth. 531.) says, "God "gave proper instruments, and appetites, to men "not for the sake of pleasure, but for the propagation "of the species. If there be any commerce with "women with any other view, the offspring will be "the bane of society. They will be wicked and "miserable, hateful to God, to demons, and to "men, and also to families and states. For this "reason," he adds, "laws were made in Greece "that men should have no commerce with their "own mothers, daughters, or sisters, nor in any "sacred place, or in public." He also says that "all commerce contrary to nature" by which he no doubt meant sodomy, "must be prevented."

Many of the sentences of Demophilus breathe such a spirit of devotion, that they are justly suspected of a purer source than any heathen philosophy. On this account I shall quote but few of them. "Do not ask of God what you cannot "keep; for no gift of God can be taken from you. "He, therefore, will not give what you cannot

"keep.

"keep........ No gift of God is greater than vir-"tue........ A frugal and poor philosopher lives a "life like to that of God, and he considers it as the "greatest wealth, that he possesses nothing exter-"nal (that is out of his control) nothing unneces-"sary. For the acquisition of riches inflames co-"vetousness, but to live well and happily nothing "is requisite but to act justly........ Being born "of God, and having our root in him, we should "adhere to it. For springs of water, and the pro-"ductions of the earth, dry up, or putrefy, when "cut off from their respective sources........ "It is impossible that the same person should be "addicted to pleasure, or the acquisition of riches, "and be devoted to God. And though he should "sacrifice hecatombs, he is the more impious, and "farther removed from religion and God." (Gale's, Op. Myth. p. 620, 625.)

But what are the best maxims, precepts, or even laws, without proper sanctions? They will be admired, and respected, by those who are previously disposed to observe them; but on others, which is the thing principally to be aimed at, they will have no effect whatever; but may even be ridiculed, and openly disregarded. And what are the proper sanctions of virtue and piety, which evidently have not always any reward in this life, but that providence of God which extends to *another*, and with this the Pythagorean philosophy was not provided.

SOCRATES AND JESUS COMPARED.

INTRODUCTION.

THE history of Socrates is so singular a phenomenon in the heathen world, and his general behaviour, and the manner of life to which he devoted himself, have in them so much that resemble those of the ancient prophets, and even of our Saviour, that they have always drawn the particular attention of the friends of divine revelation, though these have formed very different opinions on the subject.

If we look into any account of the Grecian philosophers who preceded Socrates, or who followed him (and some of the most eminent of the latter were his professed disciples) we shall find none of them to resemble him, even in the general features of his conduct, though his education as a philosopher was in all respects the same with theirs; and they all fell far short of him with respect to purity of moral character.

If we may depend upon what is transmitted to

us concerning him by Xenophon and Plato, who were his cotemporaries and disciples, both men of great eminence, (and there were no writers in the heathen world whose characters stand higher than theirs) he was a very extraordinary man with respect both to wisdom and virtue. And as Socrates had enemies as well as friends, and his accusers must have had their friends too, had the accounts of Xenophon or Plato not been in the main agreeable to truth, it would have been in our power, (as the age abounded with writers) to perceive some trace of their objections. But nothing of this kind appears.

From both these accounts we must conclude that Socrates was a man who, from early life, not only abstained from vice himself: and practised every thing that he thought to be a virtue, but one who devoted himself to the promoting of virtue in others; continually throwing himself in the way of every person whom he thought he could benefit by his exhortations or instructions;- that by this means a considerable number of young men, especially those of the best families, of much considertion and wealth, in the city of Athens, were strongly attached to him; and yet, that though he was poor

poor, and many of them were rich, he never accepted of any reward for his instructions.

In his conduct as a citizen he was most uncorrupt and fearless, risking his popularity, and even his life, rather than consent to any thing that appeared to him unjust. When he was falsely accused he behaved with the greatest magnanimity at his trial, and when sentence of death was passed upon him he yielded to it with the greatest calmness. He refused to solicit for any abatement of the sentence as a favour, and declined all the offers of his friends to assist him in an escape from prison. When the fatal cup was brought to him, he drank it with the greatest readiness and composure, and died with much apparent satisfaction.

The sentiments and principles of such a man as this, who lived in the most polished city of Greece, at a period the most distinguished for every thing that can contribute to fame, in arts, science, or policy, and yet the most addicted to idolatry of any city in Greece, certainly deserves to be investigated, and his conduct to be scrutinized; and this I shall endeavour to do in the best manner that the materials we are furnished with will enable me.

SECTION I.

Of the Polytheism and Idolatry of Socrates.

That Socrates was an idolater, or a worshipper of a multiplicity of Gods, and such as were acknowledged by his countrymen, and that he conformed in all respects to the popular modes of worship, cannot be denied. " He sacrificed, says Xe-" nophen, (p. 2.) both on the public altars of the ci-" ty, and often at his own house; and he also prac-" ticed divination in the most public manner." On trial he said, (p. 377.) " he had never sacrificed " to, or acknowledged, or sworn by, or even made " mention of, any gods but Jupiter, Juno, and o-" thers that were received by his fellow citizens. " Do not I believe," says he, (p. 3.) " that the " sun, and the moon, are gods as well as others ?" " Do we not suppose demons" (and one of these he acknowledged to have given particular attention to him) " to be either gods, or the sons of gods," (p. 21.) And in his last moments, after he had drunk the poison, recollecting a vow that he had made to sacrifice a cock to Æsculapius, he desired Crito, a pupil and particular friend of his, to discharge

charge it for him, and begged that he would not neglect to do it, (p. 186.) Though on one occasion he speaks of *one God* that constructed and preserves the world, (p. 318.) he does not say that he was the *only God.*

All heathens and idolaters, civilized or uncivilized, were addicted to divination, imagining that by this means they could pry into futurity, and find out what their gods signified by certain signs, as the flight of birds, the form of the livers of the animals they sacrificed, and many other things, which are generally considered as accidents. Socrates was so far from seeing the folly of these observances, that he was to an immoderate degree assiduous in his attention to them. Being of opinion, (p. 8.) that "the gods signified their will by divination to those whom they were disposed to favour." Whenever he was in doubt about any thing of importance, he sent some of his friends to consult the oracle (p. 5.) and he advised his friends, if they had occasion for the knowledge of any thing that they could not attain to themselves, to apply to the gods in the modes of divination, (p. 352;) Saying, that "they who would regulate either their own affairs, or those of the state, stood in need of these practices." (p. 5.)

Besides having recourse to the usual modes of divination, Socrates believed that, upon every occasion of importance, the will of the gods was signified to himself in particular, but in what manner he does not clearly say. He sometimes calls it *a voice* (Φωνη) p. 28. At his trial he said he had often been heard to say that a divine voice was frequently present with him.

Notwithstanding all this evidence of the polytheistic sentiments, and corresponding practice, of Socrates, Rollin and others suppose him to have been a believer in the *divine unity*, and to have been sensible of the absurdity and folly of all the popular superstitions, and of the popular worship of his country. But I am far from seeing any sufficient evidence of this. If he had had the weakness, which however is never ascribed to him, to conceal this before his judges, he might have avowed it before his death, bearing a dying and most honourable testimony to important truth; whereas, on both these occasions, his language and conduct were the very reverse of what, on the supposition of this superior knowledge, they ought to have been. Indeed I much question whether any person educated as Socrates was, among polytheists and

and idolaters, could possibly, by the mere light of nature, have attained to a firm belief of the divine unity, though he might in some degree have been sensible of the folly and absurdity of the prevailing superstitions.

Section II.

The Sentiments of Socrates concerning the Gods, and their Providence.

A polytheist and idolater as Socrates was, he had just and honourable sentiments concerning the divine power and providence, and of the obedience that men owe to the gods. And though his ideas on these subjects are far short of what we find in the Psalms of David, and the writings of the Hebrew prophets, they are much more rational and sublime than the opinions of the heathens in general, or those of the philosophers that followed him.

We have seen that Socrates ascribed to *a god* the formation and government of the world, whereas, according to Hesiod (whose *theogony* was, no doubt, that which was generally received by the Greeks) the world had been from eternity, and the origin of the gods was subsequent to it. Socrates points out in particular the wisdom and goodness of providence in the disposition of the different senses and the several parts of the human body, as that of the eyes, the eye-lashes, and eye-lids; and in the structure of the teeth, which in the different animals are shaped and situated in the most convenient manner, the best adapted to their respective uses (p. 62.) He had, no doubt, the same opinion of the wisdom and goodness displayed in the structure and disposition of every thing else in nature.

He, moreover, believed that the gods know every thing that is not only said or done, but that is even thought and intended, though ever so privately; being present in all places; so that, whenever they think proper, they can give intimations to man of every thing relating to them, (p. 14.). "The "deity" (το θειον) he says, (p. 65.) "sees and hears "all things, is every where present, and takes care "of all things." And he makes this obvious and practical use of the doctrine, viz. that "if men be-"lieved it, they would abstain from all base acti-"ons even in private, persuaded that nothing that "they did was unknown to the gods." (p. 70.)

The gods, he also thought, know every thing that is future, though they conceal the knowledge of those things from men in general; so that,

"though

"though a man built a house, he could not be certain that he should inhabit it, nor could a general "be sure whether it would be proper for him to "march his army, &c." (p. 6.) Agreeably to this, it was his custom, in his prayer to the gods, to request that they would grant him what was good, without specifying what he wished for; since they best knew what was so. (p. 45.) Like the heathens in general, he considered lightning as coming more immediately from the gods, as one mode of giving intimations to men. (p. 312.)

According to Socrates, it is the gods that have made the distinction between men and the inferior animals, having given them rational souls, so that they only know that there are gods, and can worship them. "There is no such principle and excellent quality," he said "in the brutes; and in "consequence of this superiority, men are like "gods with respect to other animals," (p. 66.)

Speaking of the goodness of the gods to man, he says, (p. 306.) "they supply us not only with ne-"cessaries, but with things that are adapted to give "us pleasuae." He mentions particularly as their gifts, water and fire, the grateful and useful change of the seasons, and our various senses, adapted to peculiar species of good. "This," he says, (p. 310.) "shews their concern for us."

Socrates considered all unwritten laws, obligatory on man in society, the origin of which cannot be traced, as having the gods for their authors. Among these he mentions the universal maxim, that the gods ought to be worshipped, (p. 327.) that gratitude is due to benefactors, that parents ought not to have sexual commerce with their children, and all other universally acknowledged principles of morality.

In answer to the objection from our not seeing the gods, he mentions several things in nature, the existence and powers of which cannot be denied, and which are invisible or inscrutable by us, as lightning, the wind, and the intellectual powers of man; "Thus," says he, (p. 313.) "when we see "the powers of the gods, we must reverence them, "though we do not see them."

Nothing can exceed the respect that Socrates entertained for the authority and will of the gods, whenever, and in whatever manner, it was made known. "If," says he, (p. 51.) "the gods signi- "fy their will, we must no more depart from it, "and take other counsel, than we should prefer the "conduct of a blind man, who did not know the "road,

"road, to that of one who saw it and knew it; al-"ways prefering the direction of the gods, to that "of men."

Agreeable to this, when he was addressing his judges, he said, (p. 40.) that "if they would acquit "him on condition that he would discontinue his "instructions to young persons, which he believ-"ed the gods had enjoined him, or suffer death, he "would answer that he must obey god rather than "man; and that if they should banish him to any "other country, he should think it his duty, to do "there what he had done at Athens." (p. 40.) "Whatever be the situation in which a man is plac-"ed, there, he said, he should remain at any risk, "even of life, (p. 23.) dreading baseness more "than any thing else. So the gods having, as, I "believe, placed me where I have been, and order-"ed me to remain philosophizing, and scrutinizing "myself and others, I must not desert that station, "for fear of death, or any thing else."

When Aristodemus, with whom he was discoursing on this subject, said that he did not deny that that there were gods, but he thought they were too great to stand in need of his worship, Socrates replied, (p. 64.) that the greater they were, the more they were to be honoured.

As to the manner in which the gods were to be honoured, he, like other heathens, thought it was to be determined by the laws of every particular country. But he justly thought that the satisfaction the gods received from these marks of respect did not depend upon the costliness of the sacrifices. "The offering of a poor man," he said, (p. 49) "is as acceptable to the gods, as the more expen-"sive ones of the rich."

Section III.

Of the excellent moral Character of Socrates.

These, it cannot be denied, are excellent sentiments, and much to be admired, considering the little light that Socrates had, viz. that of nature only, uninstructed by any revalation. And with him these sentiments were not merely speculative. His whole life seems to have been strictly conformable to them, being eminently virtuous, and wholly devoted to the service of his fellow citizens.

Xenophon, who knew him well (though, having been his pupil, we may suppose him to have been prejudiced in his favour) gives the following general account of his character and conduct, (p. 359.)

359.) "He was so religious that he did nothing "without the advice of the gods. He was so "just, that he never injured any person in the "smallest matter, but rendered every service in "his power to those with whom he had any con-"nection. He was so temperate that he never "preferred what was grateful to what was useful. "He was so prudent, that he never mistook the "the worse for the better; nor did he want the "advice of others, but always judged for himself. "In his conversation, he excelled in defining what "was right, and in shewing it to others, reprov-"ing the vicious, and exhorting to the practice "of virtue."

Though the circumstances of Socrates were the reverse of affluent, he would never receive any gratuity for the lessons that he gave, as all other philosophers and public teachers did; and by this means, as he said, (p. 74.) he preserved his freedom and independence. When upon his trial he was urged by his friends to supplicate the judges, as was the universal custom, in order to move their compassion, he refused to ask any favour even of them; being of opinion that this was contrary to the *laws*, according to which, and not according to *favour*, judges ought to decide, (p. 317.)

In

In all the changes in the political state of the turbulent city of Athens, which were many in the time of Socrates, he adhered inflexibly to what he thought to be just, without being influenced by hope or fear. This was particularly conspicuous on two occasions. The first was when, being one of the judges in the case of the ten generals who were tried for their lives on account of their not collecting and burying the dead after a naval engagement, and all the rest (influenced, no doubt, by the popular clamour against them) condemned them to die, he alone refused to concur in the sentence. Soon after the citizens in general, convinced of the injustice of the sentence, though after it had been carried into execution, approved of his conduct. The other was during the government of the thirty tyrants, when, though in manifest danger of his life, he refused to approve of their measures; and he escaped by nothing but their overthrow, and the city recovering its liberty.

That Socrates at the close of life expressed his satisfaction in his own conduct cannot be thought extraordinary. It was, he observed, (p. 366.) in concurrence with the general opinion of his countrymen, and with a declaration of the oracle at Delphi in his favour. For when it was consulted

by

by Chærephon, one of his disciples, the answer was, that there was no person more honorable (ἐλευθεριώτερον) more just, or more wise * than he. (p. 371.)

He put, however, a very modest construction on this oracle; which was that, though he knew no more than other men, he did not, like them, pretend to know more. (p. 9. 12.) so that he only knew himself, and his own ignorance, better than other men. His reputation in consequence of it, and of his conduct in general, had no other than the happiest influence upon him. For, addressing his judges (p. 34.) he observed, that "it be-"ing a generally received opinion, that he was wi-"ser than other men," he said that "whether that "opinion was well founded or not, he thought he "ought not to demean himself by any unworthy "action."

Notwithstanding Socrates's consciousness of integrity, and general merit, and the good opinion of the wise and virtuous, he was so sensible of the malice

* *In Xenophon the response of the oracle is expressed by* σωφρονέστερος, *but Plato always uses the word* σοφώτερος. *Cicero in referring to it uses the word* sapientissimus.

malice of his enemies, that when he was brought before his judges he had no expectation of being acquitted, and therefore he expressed his surprize when he found that he was condemned by a majority of no more than three votes, (p. 36.) out of 500.*

It being customary at Athens, when any person was found guilty of the charge brought against him, to require him to say what, in his own opinion, his punishment should be; and this question being proposed to Socrates, conscious as he was of no demerit, but on the contrary of his valuable services to his country; he said that, since he had made no gain by his profession of public instructor, had never held any lucrative office in the state, and he was poor, he was, like other persons in a similar situation, and with similar claims, entitled to a maintenance at the public expense in the Prytaneum, (p. 37.) If they destroyed him, he farther said, they would not soon find another like him, (p. 27.) This has the appearance of vanity and ostentation. But if the praising a man's self be at all justifiable, it is on such an occasion as this,

* *This, exclusive of the president, Rollin supposes to have been the number of the judges.*

this, when he is unjustly censured and condemned by others.

SECTION IV.

The Imperfection of Socrates's Ideas concerning Piety, and Virtue in general.

Just and sublime as were the sentiments that Socrates professed concerning the power and providence of the gods, and of the obligation that men are under to reverence and worship them, his ideas of the *manner* in which this was to be done were by no means such as might have been expected in consequence of them. According to him, all the duties that properly rank under the head of *piety* are the observance of the religious rites of the countries in which men live. "The gods, he, "says, (p. 338.) are not to be honoured by every "man as he pleases, but as the laws direct." This was agreeable to the answer received from Delphi, when inquiry was made concerning the manner in which men should please the gods; for the answer returned was, "by complying with the "institutions of our country," (p. 313.) After mentioning this, Socrates added, that "all states had

"had decreed that the "gods are to be placated "by sacrifices, according to the faculties of each "of them." (p. 314.)

Now, what the rites of the heathen religion were, those of Athens by no means excepted, is well known. Little did they accord with any just sentiments of what we now deem to be *piety*, i. e. a reverence for the perfections and providence of God, gratitude for his favours, submission to his will, in a strict obedience to the moral precepts he has enjoined, and confidence in his protection and favour in consequence of it. With these sentiments sacrifices, and the other rites of the heathen religions, had no connection whatever. Rather, they were the occasion, and provocatives, of licentiousness, and lewdness, as must have been well known to Socrates himself.

The moral maxims of Socrates, independent of those relating to religion, are admirable, especially his saying, (p. 83.) that "there is no "better way to true glory than to endeavour to "be good rather than seem to be so." But his general rule concerning the nature of *justice*, in which he probably included virtue in general, was that, "whatever is *lawful*," or agreeable to the laws, "is just," (p. 321. 326.) whereas, nothing

can

can be more variable than the laws of particular states, or more discordant with one another.

With respect to the subjects of religion and morals in general, Socrates always professed a greater regard to the laws than reason or good sense will justify, though he might be induced to say more on this subject in consequence of his being accused of being no friend to the popular religion, and of corrupting youth by attaching them to himself, to the neglect of their parents and others. And it is very possible that, in some of his instructions he had inculcated duties of a purer and higher kind than the institutions of his country would encourage or authorize. Such, however, might be expected from the sentiments he generally expressed.

Considering the wretched philosophy of the Sophists, whose ostentation, and absurdities, Socrates exposed, we shall not wonder at the advice he gave his hearers with respect to the principal object of their pretended science. He recommended to them the study of Geography, Astronomy, and the sciences in general, only so far as they were of practical use in life, (p. 350,) but he particularly dissuaded them from the study of *the structure of the universe*, because, he said, " it was not designed to be "discovered by man, nor could it be agreeable to "the gods to have that inquired into which they "did not make known to man." For nothing could be more presumptuous than the manner in which those Sophists, and the philosophers of those times in general, decided concerning this great subject; and with them it led to nothing of any real value with respect to men's conduct, but puffed them up with conceit, without any foundation of real knowledge. On this account he is said by Seneca to have reduced all philosophy to morals. *Totam philosophiam revocavit ad mores, Epist.* 71.

But could Socrates have seen the progress that a truer philosophy than any that existed in his time has now made, and how directly it leads to the most profound admiration of the works and providence of God, unfolding the wisdom, power, and goodness of the great creator; and had he seen the connection which this reverence for God, and consequently for his laws, has (on the system of revelation) with moral virtue, he would have been the first to lay stress upon it, and to inculcate it upon his pupils.

As the laws of his country, which with Socrates were too much the standard of right, with respect both

both to religion and morals, were very imperfect on many subjects, we do not wonder that he did not express a sufficient indignation (such as those do who are acquainted with the purer and more severe precepts of revealed religion relating to them) at some particular vices, especially sodomy, which the laws of God by Moses justly punished with death.

When Critias, then his pupil, was in love with Euthydemus, and avowedly, as it should seem, for the vilest purpose, he dissuaded him from pursuing his object; but only as a thing that was illiberal, unbecoming a man of honour and delicacy. "It "was" he said "begging of the object of his pas-"sion like a pauper, and for a thing that would do "him no good," (p. 29.) The gratification of this passion he said, resembled a hog rubbing himself against a stone, (p. 30.) This, no doubt, shews a *contempt* for this vice, but no sufficient *abhorrence* of it, as such a degradation of human nature ought to excite. When another of his pupils gave a kiss to a son of Alcibiades, who was very beautiful, he only asked whether it did not require great boldness to do it; meaning that, after this, it would not be easy to refrain from endeavouring to take greater liberties with him. There is too much of pleasantry, and too little of seriousness, in this method of considering the subject.

A similar remark may be made on the interview that Socrates had with a celebrated courtesan of the name of Theodota, whom he had the curiosity to visit on account of what he had heard of her extraordinary beauty and elegant form, so that statuaries applied to her to take models from her; and to whom the historian says she exhibited her person as much as decency would permit. In this situation Socrates and his pupils found her; but in the conversation that he had with her he discovered no just sense of the impropriety of her life and profession. She spake to him of her galants as her friends, who contributed to her support without labour, and hoped that by his recommendation she should procure more; adding, "How shall I persuade "you to this." He replies, "This you must find "out yourself, and consider in what way it may be "in my power to be of use to you." And when she desired him to come often to see her, he only jestingly said, that he was not sufficiently at leisure from other engagements. (p. 251.) Ready as Socrates was to give good advice to young men, he

said

said nothing to her to recommend a more virtuous and reputable course of life than that which he knew she led.

It was not in this manner that Jesus and his apostles would have conversed with such a person. He did not decline all intercourse with women of her character, but it was not at their houses; and what he said was intended to instruct and reclaim them. He considered them as the *sick*, and himself as the *physician*.

Women of the profession of this Theodota, if they had been well educated, were resorted to in the most open manner by men of the first character at Athens, as Aspasia by Socrates himself, and by Pericles, who afterwards married her. Nor was fornication in general, with women of that profession, at all disreputable, either in Greece, or at Rome.

How much more pure are the morals of christianity in this respect. So great, however, was the prevalence of this vice, and so little had it been considered as one, in the heathen world, that the apostle Paul, writing to the christian churches in Greece, and especially at Corinth, the richest and most voluptuous city in that part of the world, is urgent to dissuade his converts from it. See particularly (1. Cor. vi. 9. &c.) where among those who would be excluded from the kingdom of heaven, he mentions fornicators in the first place. *Know ye not, that the unrighteous shall not inherit the kingdom of God. Be not deceived; neither fornicators, nor idolaters, nor adulterers, nor effeminate, nor abusers of themselves with mankind, nor thieves, nor covetous, nor drunkards, nor revilers, nor extortioners, shall inherit the kingdom of God.*

SECTION V.

Of Socrates's Belief in a future State.

Though Socrates had more just ideas concerning the nature and character of deity, and also of the nature and obligations of virtue, than the generality of his countrymen, and even of the philosophers, he does not appear to have had any more knowledge than others concerning the great sanction of virtue, in the *doctrine of a future state.* In none of his conversations recorded by Xenophon on the subject of virtue with young men and others, is there the least mention of it, or allusion to it; which was certainly unavoidable if he had been really acquainted with it, and believed it.

Speak-

Speaking of the happiness of his virtuous pupils, he mentions the pleasure they would have in this life, and the respect that would be paid to them; and says that, "when they died they would not be "without honour, consigned to oblivion, but "would be for ever celebrated, (p. 111.") Having said this, could he have forborne to add their happier condition after death, if he had had any belief of it?

All his dissuasives from vice are grounded on some natural and necessary inconvenience to which men expose themselves by it in this life, but none of them have any respect to another. Thus he represents intemperate persons as slaves to their appetites, (p. 322.) and treating of what he considered as being the laws of nature, and therefore as those of the gods, as the prohibition of marriage between parents and their children, (p. 328.) he only says that "the offspring of such a mixture is bad, "one of the parties being too old to produce "healthy children;" and this reason does not apply to the case of brothers and sisters. Another law of nature, he says, is to do good in return for good received; but the penalty of not doing it he makes to be nothing more than being deserted by a man's friends when he will have the most want of them, and to be forced to apply to those who have no friendship for him. (p. 329.)

It is particularly remarkable that nothing that Xenophon says as coming from Socrates, not only in his conversations with his pupils, but even at his trial, and the scenes before his death, implies a belief of a future state. All that we have of this kind is from Plato; and though he was present at the trial, and therefore what he says is, no doubt, entitled to a considerable degree of credit, it wants the attestation of *another witness*; and the want of that of Xenophon is something more than *negative;* especially as it is well known that Plato did not scruple to put into the mouth of Socrates language and sentiments that never fell from him, as it is said Socrates himself observed, when he was shewn the dialogue entitled *Lysis*, in which he is the principal speaker, as he is in many others.

In Plato's celebrated dialogue intitled *Phædo*, in which he makes Socrates advance arguments in proof of a future state, we want the evidence of some person who was present; for Plato himself was at that time confined by sickness, (P. p. 74.) so that it is very possible, as nothing is said of it by Xeno-

Xenophon, that he might not have held any discourse on the subject at all.

Besides, all that Socrates is represented by Plato to have said on this subject is far from amounting to any thing like certain *knowledge*, and real *belief*, with respect to it, such as appears in the discourses of Jesus, and the writings of the apostles. Socrates, according to Plato, generally speaks of a future state, and the condition of men in it, as the *popular belief*, which might be true or false. "If" says he (p. 46) "what is said be true, we shall in another state die no more. In death" he says to "his judges" (p. 44.) "we either lose all sense of "things, or, *as it is said*, go into some other place; "and if so, it will be much better; as we shall be "out of the power of partial judges, and come before those that are impartial. Minos, Rhadamanthus, Æacus, Triptolemus, and others, who "were demigods." Taking his leave of them, he "says, I must now depart to die, while you continue in life; but which of these is better, the gods "only can tell; for in my opinion no man can "know this."

This certainly implies no faith on which to ground real practice, from which a man could, with the apostle, *live as seeing things invisible*, being

ing governed by a regard to them more than to things present, the one as certain as the other, and infinitely superior in value, *the things that are seen being temporary, while those that are unseen are eternal.* (2. Cor. iv. 10.)

Notwithstanding this uncertainty of Socrates with respect to a future state, he died with great composure and dignity; considering his death at that time as, on the whole, better for him than to live any longer in the circumstances in which, at his time of life (being seventy years old) he must have lived; especially as a coward, discovering unmanly dread of death, in exile and disgrace; dying also without torture, surrounded by his friends, and admirers, who would ensure his fame to the latest posterity.

That such *arguments* in proof of a future state as Plato puts into the mouth of Socrates should really have been advanced, and have have any stress laid upon them, by him, in so serious a time as just before his death, is exceedingly improbable, from the extreme futility of them. They are more like the mere play of imagination, than the deductions of reason.

His first argument is, that as every thing else in nature has its contrary, *death* must have it also, and

and if so, it must be followed by *life*, as day follows night, and a state of *vigilance* always follows *sleep*. (p. 56.). But might it not be said that, for the same reason, every thing that is *bitter* must some time or other become *sweet*, and every thing that is sweet become bitter?

His second argument is, that all our present acquired knowledge is only the recollection of what we knew before in a former state. (p. 100.) But what evidence is there of this?

His third argument is, that only compound substances are liable to corruption, by a separation of the parts of which they consist; but the mind is a simple substance, and therefore cannot be affected by the dissolution of the body in death. (p. 111.) This is certainly the most plausible argument of the three, but it is of too subtle a nature to give much satisfaction. If the mind have several powers and affections, and be furnished with a multiplicity of ideas, there is the same evidence of its being a compound as there is with respect to the body; and if the power of thinking, or *mental action*, bear any resemblance to corporeal *motion*, it may cease, and be suspended, though the substance remain.

Are these sufficient arguments for a man at the point

point of death to build his faith and hope upon? As this appears to have been all that the most sagacious of the heathens could attain to by the light of nature, what reason have we to be thankful for the superior light of revelation, and especially for the gospel, which *brings life and immortality to light.* (2. Tim. i. 10.)

Socrates does not, in this celebrated dialogue, make any mention of the argument from the *universal belief* of a future state, as handed down by *tradition* in all nations; which, though far short of a proper *proof* of the doctrine, is more plausible than any of the three arguments above mentioned. For it might be presumed that the ancestors of the human race, from whom the tradition descended to their posterity, had some proper evidence of what they delivered, though that had not been preserved, the doctrine itself only being retained. This, indeed, seems to have been the case with respect to the Jews. Though they were in the time of our Saviour firm believers in the doctrine of a resurrection, the record of the revelation (for it could not have come from any other source) had been long lost.

How far short is every thing that Socrates is represented as saying of the perfect assurance with which

which Jesus always spoke of his resurrection to an immortal life, and of the glory that was prepared for him in the councils of God from the foundation of the world; when, as the writer of the epistle to the Hebrews says (c. xii. 20.) *for the joy that was set before him, he endured the cross, despising the shame, and is set down at the right hand of the throne of God.* How short it falls of the confidence which the apostle Paul, in the near view of death, expresses with respect to *his* future prospects, (2. Tim. iv. 7.) *I have fought the good fight, I have finished my course, I have kept the faith. Henceforth there is laid up for me a crown of righteousness, which the Lord, the righteous judge, will give me at that day; and not to me only, but to all them that love his appearing.* With what satisfaction and joy have thousands of christian martyrs relinquished this life in the assurance of a better.

Besides, after all that Socrates advances in proof of a future state, he seems to make it the peculiar privilege of those who apply to philosophy, who have in some degree abstracted the purer mind from the gross body by intense meditation. (p. 83.) "This," he says, (p. 94.) "was intended by the "authors of the *mysteries* when they said that none "besides the *initiated* would live with the gods af- "ter

"ter death; for that by the initiated were meant "those who philosophized in a right manner (ορθως) "and that whether he had succeeded or not, it had "been his endeavour through life to do so."

According to this, the great mass of mankind have no more interest in a future state than brute animals. But the gospel makes no difference in favour of philosophers, or any other class of men. According to this, *all that are in the graves shall hear the voice of the son of man*, (John. v. 28.) *and shall come forth; they that have done good to the resurrection of life, and they that have done evil to the resurrection of condemnation.* Then too (Rev. xx. 15.) *the sea shall give up the dead that is in it, and every man shall be judged according to his works.*

SECTION VI.

Of the Dæmon of Socrates.

Much has been advanced on the subject of the *dæmon*, as it is commonly called, of Socrates, or that *divine voice*, as he termed it, which gave him warnings about what he was about to do, if it was impro-

improper for him, and which was evidently something different from *divination*, to which he often had recourse, or from any casual *omen* that might occur to him. This he said had accompanied him from his youth; but though it forbad him to do certain things that he was deliberating about, it had never prompted him to any particular action. *(ib.)* This divine voice did not respect his own conduct only, but sometimes that of others; and he declared that whenever he had, from this warning, signified the will of the gods to any of his friends, he had never been deceived by it. (p. 370.)

Speaking of his general manner of life, and plan of conduct, in devoting his time and talents to the instruction of others, he said, (p. 32.) it had been enjoined him "by the gods, by oracles, by the "god" (probably meaning that particular deity from whom he had the hints above mentioned) "by "dreams, and every other mode in which, by di-"vination, they order things to be done." This was said by him in his address to his judges; and he added that, though the deity had checked him in the smallest things that he was about to do, if they were improper (p. 44.) yet that when he was thinking of his defence, the deity had thus forbidden

him

him to make any, and this not only once, but twice, (p. 365.) nor, while he was then speaking did he perceive any check with respect to any part of his conduct. (p. 44.) He therefore concluded that, since this divine voice had not interfered on this occasion, it was best for him to await the sentence of his judges, though they should condemn him to death. "The situation I am now in," he said, "did not come to me by chance; for nothing can happen amiss to a good man with respect to life or death; since the gods never neglect him. It is, therefore, better for me to die now, and to be exempt from all farther labours." (p. 47.)

These intimations, in whatever manner they were communicated, are now, I believe, generally thought to have been a mere *illusion*, when nothing really supernatural took place. Had these suggestions occurred only once or twice in the course of his life, the hypothesis of their being an illusion, or mere imagination, might have been admitted. But they had attended him, he said, from his youth, and had given him hints not only respecting his own conduch (which by his account had been very frequent) but sometimes that of his friends; and because he had received no check from this quarter with

with respect to his conduct at his trial, he concluded with certainty that it was right, and would have the best issue.

Besides the admonitions of this kind which were communicated while he was awake, he had others he says, given him in dreams. One of these he mentioned just before his death; which was that he should apply to music. On this he had put various constructions; and lest he should not have hit upon the true meaning of it, he composed while he was in prison, a hymn in praise of Apollo, and turned some of the fables of Æsop into verse, which were always recited in a musical recitative. (p. 77.)

This might have been nothing more than a common dream, on which he put an uncommon construction, in consequence of imagining that there was something supernatural in it. But this could not have been the case with respect to the hints that he received when he was awake, whether by the medium of a real voice, or in any other way.

In no other respect does Socrates appear to have been an enthusiast. On the contrary, he was a man of a calm and even temper, not distinguished by any peculiarity of behaviour, or extravagance of any kind. And though he seems to have addressed himself to every person to whom he imagined that his advice would be useful, he was never charged with being impertinent, so as to give offence to any. On the contrary, his address was insinuating and pleasing; so that his hearers in general were delighted with his conversation, and this through the course of a long life.

Since, then, he persisted in his account of these admonitions to the last, and in the most serious situation that a man could be in, and his veracity was never questioned, though I am far from forming any fixed opinion on a subject of so great obscurity, I think it may admit of a doubt, whether they may not be supposed to have come, in whatever manner they were given, from God. I do not see any thing unworthy of the Divine Being in his distinguishing this extraordinary man in this way. Being no judge of the propriety of the divine conduct, we must be determined in every case of this kind by the *evidence of facts*, according to the established rules of estimating the value of testimony in general.

These admonitions are said to have been proper to the occasions on which they were delivered; so that leading to *good*, if they came from any superior being, it must have been a wise and benevolent

one.

one. They would, therefore, tend to impress the mind of Socrates, and those of his numerous disciples and admirers, with an idea of the existence of a power superior to man, though not in a manner so decisive and convincing as the express revelations that were made to the Hebrew prophets. But why it should please God to distinguish any one man, or any particular nation, with his peculiar gifts, and in what degree he should do this, is not for us to say. If we see good to result from it, we ought not to cavil or complain, but be satisfied, and thankful.

That in any manner whatever, and in what degree soever, it shall appear that the maker of the world gives attention to it, it is a proof of the reality of a *providence* in general, and of the divine interference out of the usual course of the laws of nature. It is therefore a decisive proof of a great and important truth. And if he be not such a god as Epicurus and other philosophers supposed, one who, (whether he had created the world or not) sat a perfectly unconcerned spectator of all that passed in it, but really interested himself in the affairs of men by occasional interpositions, it cannot be doubted but that, from the same principle, he does it at all

 times,

times, though in a manner less apparent; and that his final treatment of men will be according to his proper character, whatever that be, if he be a righteous and good being, he will, no doubt, most approve of virtue and goodness in men, and show it by rewarding the righteous and punishing the wicked.

The reason why he does not do this completely at present, though we are not without some intimations of his *disposition* to do so, it is not difficult to account for. There must be time and opportunity to form characters. The existence of vice, as well as of virtue, in the world is necessary for this purpose; and it is not till a character be properly formed that a suitable treatment can be adjusted to it. If our maker think of us at all, it must be for our good.

Thus do such supernatural suggestions as Socrates asserts that he had afford some obscure and indistinct evidence of a *moral government of the world*, and consequently of a future state of righteous retribution. Why such intimations were not more frequent, more distinct, or more general, is beyond our comprehension. If we be asked why the wise and benevolent author of nature permitted the rise and long continuance of the most absurd

and

and abominable systems of polytheism and idolatry to prevail so long in the world, or why he should suffer so much vice and misery to exist in it at present; why mankind should be afflicted with war, pestilence, and famine, and be subject to such distressful accidents as lightning, hurricanes, and earthquakes, we can only say with Abraham of old, (Gen. xviii. 25.) that the *maker and judge of the earth will do what is right;* and therefore that all these evils, repugnant as they seem to our ideas of benevolence, may hereafter appear to have been the best methods of promoting general and lasting happiness.

If the present state be considered as nothing more than the *infancy* of our being, we may naturally expect to be no more able to account for our treatment in it, than a child is able to account for that of its parent, who, though ever so affectionate, must, if he be wise, continually do what the child, cannot see any reason for, and what he must think to be very often exceedingly harsh and unreasonable. And as appearances in nature, and in the structure of the world, furnish an unquestionable proof of a wise and benevolent author, the present imperfect state of virtue and happiness does, as such, afford some evidence that this *is* the infant state of our being; and is therefore an argument, and a promise, as we may say, of future good. And slight as it may be, and less satisfactory than we could wish, it should be highly grateful and acceptable to us.

Section VII.

Of the Character, and Teaching, of Socrates compared with those of Jesus

When we consider what was most obvious in the general disposition and behaviour of Socrates and of Jesus, we see no apparent difference with respect to the command of their natural appetites and passions, or their temper in general. Both were equally temperate, though as Jesus was not married, and was never charged with incontinence, he shewed a command of his natural passions in this respect for which there was no occasion in the case of Socrates. Both of these men seem to have been equally free from austerity and moroseness in their general behaviour, being equally affable, and no enemies to innocent festivity on proper occasions.

They

They were both capable of strong personal attachments, as Socrates to several of his friends and pupils, and Jesus to the family of Lazarus, to his apostles in general, and to John in particular. And his discourses and prayer before his death shows his affection for them in the strongest manner. Also his attention to his mother, while hung upon the cross, deserves particular notice in this respect.

Both of them were the friends of virtue, and laboured to promote it; but Jesus expressed stronger indignation against vice, especially the vices of the great, and of the leading men of his country, against whose pride, hypocrisy, and injustice, he pronounced the most vehement and provoking invectives; whereas Socrates adopted the gentler method of irony and ridicule.

There was, I doubt not, great propriety, as well as ingenuity, in the ironical manner that Socrates is said to have very often used, in exposing the vices of particular persons; and by this means he is said, and with great probability, to have made himself many bitter enemies. But there was certainly more of *dignity* in the direct and serious invectives of Jesus, such as his saying, (Mat. xxiii. 13. &c.) *Woe unto you Scribes and pharisees, hypocrites, &c.*

And let it not be forgotten that this was pronounced by the son of a carpenter, of only about thirty years of age, and publicly in the temple, where he was always attended by great multitudes of persons of all ranks, and that no reply was ever made to him on these occasions. He by this conduct made himself as many enemies as Socrates, but it was in a manner that showed more courage.

Both Jesus and Socrates took advantage of present incidents, as hints for their instructive discourses; but those of Socrates have the appearance of having been contrived before hand, while those to which Jesus alluded were such as naturally presented themselves at the time.

What was peculiar to Socrates was his proposing to his hearers a series of *questions*, by means of which he made the conclusions he wished to have drawn seem to be their own; so that all objections were precluded. A great peculiarity in the discourses of Jesus, though his manner was very various, and often authoritatively didactic, which that of Socrates never was, consisted in his numerous *parables*, the meaning of which, when he intended it to be so, was sufficiently obvious, and peculiarly striking; as in those of the rich man and Lazarus, of the man who was robbed, and nearly murdered,

on

on his way to Jericho, and the peculiarly fine one of the prodigal son, and therefore more easily retained in memory, as well as adapted to make a stronger impression on the mind, than a moral lesson not so introduced and accompanied.

At other times there was an intended obscurity in the parables and sayings of Jesus. He did not always wish to be understood at the time, but to have what he said to be remembered, and reflected upon afterwards. Such sayings were calculated to engage more attention from their being expressed in a concise, figurative and enigmatical manner; as when he said, (John ii. 19.) *Destroy this temple and in three days I will raise it up.* Such a saying as this would not be forgotten. His enemies, we find, remembered it, and his friends would understand his meaning in due time; as they would his saying, (John xii. 31.) *If I be lifted up from the earth I will draw all men unto me;* in which he alluded both to his crucifixion, his resurrection, and the universal spread of his gospel.

It is very remarkable that there are not in the most elaborate compositions of the antients or moderns any parables so excellent for pertinency to the occasion on which they were delivered, for propriety and consistency in their parts, and for important meaning, as those of Jesus. Numerous as they are, they all appear to have been unpremeditated, as they arose from circumstances in which the speaker had no choice. There is nothing trifling or absurd in any of them; and few others, though the result of much study, are free from objection of this kind. It will not be supposed that the parables of Jesus received any improvement from the writers of his life, and yet the more they are studied the more admirable they are found to be.*

Both the discourses and the general manner of life of Socrates and Jesus have an obvious resemblance, as they both went about graciously doing good, according to their several abilities, situations, and opportunities; but we see an infinite superiority with respect to Jesus, though he had no such advantage

* On this subject of parables, and every thing relating to the *internal evidences of christianity*, I would particularly recommend a most comprehensive and excellent work of Mr. J. Simpson's, entitled, *Internal and presumptive evidences of Christianity considered separately, and as united to form one argument*, 1801.

advantage of education and instruction as Socrates had.

Socrates had all the advantage that education, in the most polished city of Greece, and the most improved period of it, could give him; having been enabled by the generosity of a wealthy citizen to attend the lectures of all the celebrated masters of his time, in every branch of science then known: and with respect to natural capacity, he was probably equal to Jesus, or any other man.

On the contrary, the circumstances of the parents of Jesus, and his low occupation till he appeared in public, exclude the supposition of his having had any advantage of liberal education. This, indeed, was objected to him by his adversaries. (John vii. 15.) *The jews marvelled, saying, How knoweth this man letters, having never learned,* that is, how did he acquire so much knowledge, without being regularly instructed by the professed teachers of the law?

Notwithstanding this great disadvantage; we find that, without any previous preparation that was visible, Jesus, from his very first appearance, assumed more authority, as a teacher and reprover of vice, than any other man before or since; addressing

dressing himself to great multitudes, or single persons, the most eminent for their rank or knowledge, without the least embarrassment, and with an air of superiority to all men; and yet without the appearance of any thing impertinent, ostentatious, or insulting.

Had Socrates introduced any of his instructions with *Verily, verily, I say unto you*, or any language of a similar import, he would have exposed himself to the ridicule of his audience, even in the latest period of his life, when he had acquired the greatest respect and authority. But this language was usual with Jesus from the very first; as in his discourse on the mount, when, instead of being insulted, he by this very means excited the greater veneration and attachment. For we read, (Matt. vii. 28.) *It came to pass when Jesus had ended these sayings, the people were astonished at his doctrine, for he taught them as one having authority, and not as the scribes.*

How must any other man than Jesus have exposed himself to ridicule, if, when speaking of the Ninevites repenting at the preaching of Jonah, and of the queen of Sheba coming from her own distant country to hear the wisdom of Solomon, he had added,

ded, as Jesus did, *but a greater than Jonah*, and one *greater than Solomon is here*, (Matt. xii. 41. &c.) But for any thing that appears he was heard with the greatest awe and respect. Infinitely more arrogant must it have appeared in any other man to say, as he did, after his resurrection, (Matt. xxviii. 18.) *All power is given unto me in heaven and in earth. Go ye, therefore, and teach all nations.* No man but one who had actually risen from the dead, and who had before this performed such miracles as convinced his hearers that he had a commission from God, could have used such language as this, and have been heard with acquiescence and respect.

To say nothing on the subject of miracles, to which Socrates did not pretend (but the truth of which in the case of Jesus can alone account for the air of superior dignity and authority that he constantly assumed, as a messenger from God, and having his authority delegated to him) his discourses relate to subjects of infinitely more importance than those of Socrates, the great object of them being to inculcate a purer and more sublime morality respecting God and man than any heathen could have a just idea of, and urging his hearers in all their behaviour in this life to have a principal respect to another, which was to commence when he

himself,

himself, after a painful death, to which he knew that he was destined, and his removal from the world, should return, invested with power to raise the dead, and to judge the world, when he would give to every man according to his works.

These are pretensions that no other man besides Jesus ever made; but with these ideas of his present power from God, and his future great destination, his conduct, and his language, as a public teacher corresponded; and his hearers, believing this, heard him with suitable reverence and respect.

What other man, to mention but one instance more, would not have exposed himself to ridicule by making such pretensions, and using such language, as the following, (John xi. 25.) *I am the resurrection and the life. He that believeth in me, though he were dead, yet shall he live.* (vi. 40.) *This is the will of him that sent me, that every one who seeth the son, and believeth on him, shall have everlasting life; and I will raise him up at the last day.* (Matt. xxv. 31.) *When the son of man* (by which phrase he always meant himself) *shall come in his glory, and all his holy angels with him, then shall he sit on the throne of his glory; and before him will be gathered all nations, and he will separate them*

them one from another, as a shepherd divideth the sheep from the goats, &c.

The most astonishing proof of extraordinary authority assumed and exercised, by Jesus was his driving the buyers and sellers out of the outer court of the temple at the time of a public festival, when that use had, of course, been made of it time immemorial, and with the permission of the rulers of the nation. This he did with only a whip of small cords to drive out the oxen and other cattle; when as we read, (Mark xi. 15. *He overthrew the tables of the money changers, and the seats of them that sold doves; saying; It is written, My house shall be called the house of prayer for all nations, but ye have made it a den of thieves.* This was done without opposition, remonstrance, or delay.

When this was done the scribes and pharisees asked him by what authority he had done it, and *who gave him that authority;* but they declining to answer a question that he put to them, he refused to give them any answer. We do not, I will venture to say, in all history, read of an act of authority equal to this by any private person, and a person without any relations or patrons conspicuous for wealth or power; and yet this bold unauthorized action was never alleged against him as a breach of of the peace, or produced against him at his trial. We only read (Mark xi. 18.) that *the scribes and chief priests heard it, and sought how they might destroy him. For they feared him, because all the people were astonished at his doctrine.*

But independently of this superior *authority* with which Jesus always delivered himself, the *subjects* of his discourses and exhortations were far more serious and weighty than those of Socrates. Indeed, some of those that are recorded by Xenophon are so exceedingly trifling, that we cannot help wondering that a writer of such judgment and good sense should have thought it worth his while to relate them. Some of those of Jesus are, no doubt, of much less importance than others; as when he advises persons how to place themselves at table where there are many guests of different ranks, &c. and observations and advices of far less importance than even this are not unbecoming Socrates, Jesus, or any man in proper circumstances. For the gravest characters are not always speaking, as we say, *ex cathedra.* In the ordinary situations of human life, when nothing very serious is expected, but mere good humour and good sense, even innocent pleasantry is well received.

But

But the great inferiority in all heathens with respect to *knowledge*, especially concerning God, providence, and a future state, made it absolutely impossible that the moral discourses of Socrates should have the clearness, the weight, and importance, of those of Jesus. The comparison of their discourses in this respect shews the great superiority of the system of religious truth that was familiar to all Jews, as contained in their sacred books, to any thing that was known to the most enlightened of the heathens, among whom Socrates shines with a distinguished preeminence.

To resort once more to the conduct of Socrates and Jesus. Socrates behaved with great propriety and dignity at his trial; but it was by no means equal to the behaviour of Jesus in similar circumstances, though it is probable that he was wholly unacquainted with the forms and solemnity of courts of justice, especially those of the Romans, which would have thrown many persons intirely off their guard; whereas Socrates had himself sat as a judge in one of the most important criminal causes that was ever brought before any court of justice. But Jesus replied to the interrogations of Pilate the Roman governor, as well as to those of the

Jewish high priest, with the greatest presence of mind, and the utmost propriety; having the prudence and self command, to make no answer at all to questions that were improper, and required none. This he did in a manner that astonished Pilate himself.

The readiness of Jesus to die after a hasty and most unjust condemnation, was certainly not less to be admired than that of Socrates, though the death of the latter was the easiest possible, and not in the least disreputable; being that to which the first citizens in the state, if sentenced to die, were brought: whereas that to which Jesus was sentenced was at the same time the most painful and the most ignominious.

Socrates had a very humane and compassionate person to administer the poison to him, shedding tears when he delivered it; and with great propriety Socrates spoke kindly to him on the occasion. But it is most probable that the Roman soldiers who nailed Jesus to the cross did that office as they generally did, without any feeling of compassion, and perhaps with mockery, as they had treated him before. And yet it is probable that at the very time when they were putting him to the greatest pain,

pain, he pronounced that admirable prayer in their favour, (Luke xxiii. 24.) *Father forgive them, for they know not what they do*, there being no particular guilt in their doing that office.

Rousseau, though an unbeliever, was struck with the great difference between the cases of Jesus and Socrates in their last moments, and describes them in the following energetic manner. "The "death of Socrates, who breathed his last in philo-"sophical conversation with his friends, is the "mildest death that nature could desire; while "the death of Jesus, expiring in torment, injured, "inhumanly treated, mocked, and cursed by an "assembly of people, is the most horrible one that "a mortal could apprehend. Socrates while he "takes the poisoned cup gives his blessing to the "person who presents it to him with the tenderest "marks of sorrow, Jesus in the midst of his ago-"nies prays—for whom? for his executioners. "Ah! if the life and death of Socrates carry the "marks of a sage, the life and death of Jesus pro-"claim a God."

Section VIII.

Of the different Objects of the Instructions of Socrates and of Jesus.

There is a remarkable difference between the general conduct of Jesus and his apostles, and that of Socrates and the Grecian philosophers in general, with respect to the persons to whom they usually addressed their instructions. All the teaching of the latter was confined to persons of good condition, such as were likely to have influence in the important offices and concerns of the state; but this was no particular object with Jesus. Though Socrates, unlike other philosophers, took no money for his instructions, his admonitions appear to have been confined to persons of the same class with the pupils of the others. There is not one of the dialogues in which he is the speaker, either in Xenophon or Plato, in which the common people are any part of the audience; so that the great mass of citizens could not receive any benefit from his teaching.

On the other hand, the discourses of Jesus were addressed to persons of all ranks promiscuously, and

and generally to crowds of the common people, though without excluding any, and rather selecting those of the lower classes, who were held in contempt by the learned scribes and pharisees, for his audience. He was commonly attended by great multitudes, of whom very few can be thought to have been what we call *persons of condition*, or who were likely to have any influence in public affairs, to which indeed his instructions had no relation whatever.

On two occasions, when crowds of this kind attended him, he fed them by a benevolent miracle; whereas had they been opulent, they would, no doubt, have come sufficiently provided with every thing. We read (Mark vi. 34.) *that he was moved with compassion towards the multitude, because they were as sheep not having a shepherd.* And again, (Matt. xv. 32.) he says, *I have compassion on the multitude, because they have continued with me now three days, and have nothing to eat; and I am unwilling to send them away fasting, lest they faint in the way.*

Sometimes persons of better condition, and of a higher rank, such as Nicodemus, applied to Jesus; but we never find that he sought their society; or first, in any manner, applied to them, or to any of the scribes and pharisees, who were the leading men in the country. Whereas, Socrates with the best views, no doubt, appears to have applied to no other. In this circumstance, however, we see a striking difference between these two teachers of virtue. The object of Socrates was the instruction of a *few*, but that of Jesus of the *many*, and especially those of the middle and lower classes, as standing in most need of instruction, and most likely to receive it with gratitude and without prejudice.

The apostles, in this and in every thing else, followed the example of their master, and addressed themselves to all classes of men without distinction, and without ever selecting the powerful, the rich, or the learned. To them men of all descriptions were equal, as standing in the same relation to the common parent of all mankind; equally training up by him in the same great school of moral discipline here, and alike *heirs of immortality* hereafter.

Thus the apostle Paul says, (1 Cor. xii. 13.) *We are all baptized into one body, whether we be Jews or Gentiles, whether we be bond or free.* (Gal. xiii. 27.) *As many of you as have been baptized into Christ have put on Christ. There is neither Jew*

Jew nor Greek, there is neither bond nor free, there is neither male nor female, for ye are all one in Christ Jesus. (Col. iii. 11.) *There is neither Greek nor Jew, circumcision nor uncircumcision, barbarian, Scythian, bond nor free; but Christ is all and in all.* This is language suited to the equal nature, and equal rights of all men; but it was never held by the Grecian philosophers, nor did their conduct at all correspond to it. With them barbarians, and especially slaves, were of little account, any farther than they were qualified to serve them.

Accordingly, we find that the schools of the Grecian philosophers were attended by none but persons of considerable rank and wealth. The lower order of the citizens took no interest in any thing that they taught, so that their morals could not be at all improved by them. But by the preaching of the apostles a great and visible reformation was made among all ranks of men, and especially the lower, and of those some of the most depraved. Thus the apostle Paul, after observing what was quoted from him before, concerning those who should *not inherit the kingdom of God*, as idolaters, adulterers, thieves, &c. adds, *but such were some of you, But ye are washed, but ye are sanctified, but ye are justified, in the name of the Lord Jesus, and by*

 the

the spirit of our God. Many passages in the epistles of the apostles shew the wretched state with respect to morals in which the gospel found men, and how much they were improved by it.

In none of the dialogues of Socrates do we find any *woman* to be present, except Theodota, the courtezan above mentioned; and though the domestic manners of the Grecian women of virtue, and of condition, were such as that they could not with decency attend public discourses, the middle and lower classes of women in Greece, as in all other countries, went abroad as openly as men; and therefore might have been in the way of instruction, had the common people in general been addressed by the philosophers.

But christian teachers never made any account of difference of sex. When Jesus fed the five thousand, and also the four thousand, there were *women and children* among them, as well as men. The same was the case with the christian churches in Corinth, and other cities of Greece. Even at Athens, where Paul did not make many converts, there was one woman of the name of Damaris, (Acts xvii. 34.) What her condition was is not said. But as she is mentioned by name, it is

probable

probable that, like Lydia, she was of some considerable rank, at least her own mistress, not subject to the controul of another.

Section IX.

Inferences to be drawn from the Comparison of Socrates and Jesus.

1. In comparing the characters, the moral instructions, and the whole of the history, of Socrates and Jesus, it is, I think, impossible not to be sensibly struck with the great advantage of revealed religion, such as that of the Jews and the christians, as enlightening and enlarging the minds of men, and imparting a superior excellence of character. This alone can account for the difference between Socrates and Jesus, and the disciples of each of them; but this one circumstance is abundantly sufficient for the purpose.

The manner in which the mind of Jesus must have been impressed by the persuasion that he had of his peculiar relation to God on the one part, and to all mankind on the other, could not fail to make him superior to Socrates, or any other man, in elevation of mind, what ever might be their superiority with respect to intellect, general knowledge, or natural advantages of any other kind.

The far greater extent of the views of Jesus, as bearing an important relation to all mankind, and the most distant generations of them; being their *prophet* and *king*, and also his own peculiar relation to God, the common parent of them all, being, as it were, his *vicegerent upon earth*, necessarily gave him an elevation of character that neither Socrates nor any other man could have.

Interested as he was for all that should ever bear the christian name (which in due time he did not doubt would be the case with all men) with what fervour did he pray, (John xvii. 21.) that they might be *one with him and his Father, as they two were one*, and that they might share in *the glory that was destined for himself from the foundation of the world*. What dignity, as well as piety, do we see here? What other man could have used such language as this?

The habitual piety of Jesus was such as could not have been expected in Socrates, or the most virtuous of the heathens. He appears to have spoken, and acted, as at all times not only in the immediate presence, but as by the immediate direction of God. The *words that he spake*, he said, (John

xiv. 10.)

xiv. 10.) *were not his own, but those of the Father who sent him;* and who, being always with him, and always hearing him, performed the miraculous works by which his divine mission was evidenced. So assiduous was he in the discharge of his high commission, that, as he said, (John iv. 34.) it was *his meat and drink to do the will of his heavenly father*, and *finish the work that he gave him to do.*

Raised as he was to a preeminence above all other men, he seems to have been even more than any other man sensible of his dependence upon God, and he had recourse to him on all occasions. We even read (Luke vi. 12.) of his spending *a whole night in prayer to God;* and it was in obedience to his will that, notwithstanding the dread that he naturally felt for the painful death to which he was destined, and the horror that he expressed on the near view of it, he voluntarily and patiently submitted to it. He prayed, and with peculiar earnestness, that the bitter cup might pass from him, but immediately added, (Matt. xxvi. 39.) *Not my will but thine be done.* Nothing like this could be expected from Socrates, or any heathen. Their knowledge of God, his providence, and his will, were too obscure and uncertain for the purpose, though they had been ever so well disposed.

As

As the worship of Socrates was, nominally at least, directed only to Jupiter, Juno, and the other gods that were acknowledged by his country, it was hardly possible for him not to retain such ideas as were generally entertained of them; and notwithstanding his endeavours to divest his mind of every thing in their character that must have appeared unworthy of divinity, such is the power of association, that it was impossible he should ever do it completely; and if not, his reverence for the objects of his worship must have fallen infinitely short of that which Jesus, and the Jews in general, had for their God; and every sentiment of devotion must have partaken of that imperfection. Their love, or attachment to them, their dread of their power, their devotedness to their will in doing, and their resignation to their will in suffering, the sense they had of their constant dependence upon them, and of their presence with them, must have been very little compared with the same sentiments in the mind of a pious Jew, with respect to the one great object of his worship.

This must be apparent to any person who will read the book of Psalms, and compare those devotional compositions with any (if there be any such) of a similar nature composed by heathens. But there

there was nothing in the religions of the heathens, at least among the Greeks and Romans, that could inspire any sentiments that deserve to be called *devotional.* This striking difference no person will say was owing to any superiority of genius in the Hebrew poets, and therefore it must have been owing to superior knowledge; and this superior knowledge could not have had any source but from divine revelation. Without this the Hebrews would, no doubt, have been as absurdly superstitious as any of the neighbouring nations; and consequently their ideas of the power and providence of God as little proper to inspire sentiments of true devotion.

To persons of reflection, and acquainted with the state of the heathen world, and especially their turn of thinking and acting with respect to religion, there needs no other evidence of the truth of revelation than a comparison of the hymns in honour of the heathen gods by Callimachus, and other Grecian poets, or the *carmen seculare* of Horace, with the psalms of David, and other devotional parts of the books of scripture, with respect to justness and elevation of sentiment, and correspondent sublimity of language.

2. In

2. In the account that we have of the dæmon of Socrates, what he says of it himself, and what appears to have been generally thought of it by others, we clearly perceive that there is nothing so naturally incredible as modern unbelievers represent with respect to divine interpositions, either in the case of the vulgar, or the philosophers of ancient times. The universal practice of having recourse to oracles and divination, is alone an abundant proof of this with respect to mankind in general; and the idea of a *mystical union with God*, and a consequent intimate communication with him, came into christianity from the later Platonists. In every thing of this kind the emperors Marcus Aurelius and Julian, the great boasts of modern unbelievers, were as credulous as the lowest of the vulgar.

Where, indeed, can be the impropriety, or improbability, of the Being that made the world, giving attention to it, and giving suitable intimations of that attention; and this no uniform appearances will do. It is not men's seeing the sun rise and set, or their observing the regular changes of the seasons, that impresses them with the idea of any thing supernatural; but unusual appearances, though equally natural, arising from the same principles and laws of nature, such as thunder, lightning,

ning, eclipses, and earthquakes, &c. Both history and daily observation is a proof of this. And, surely miracles, performed by duly authorized prophets, do this infinitely better than any merely unusual natural phenomena.

This opinion of the natural incredibility of accounts of miracles, on which Mr. Hume, and after him other unbelievers lay so much stress, as what no positive testimony can shake, is quite a modern thing. But had this incredibility had any foundation in nature, it must have been the same at all times, and in all countries; and it must have affected all classes of men, princes and peasants, the learned and the unlearned; whereas all history shews that a propensity to believe accounts of divine interpositions has been universal. It entered into all systems of religion whatever, and no nation was ever without some religion. It is impossible, therefore, not to conclude that a system which supposes miracles is naturally adapted to gain belief, and therefore that a pretension to miracles is far from being a circumstance unfavourable to its reception. It is rather a presumption in its favour. If it be any object with the Divine Being to give mankind intimations of his attention to them, and govern-

government over them, which no person can say is impossible, or improbable, he could not take any other method than that of miracles to gain his end.

Much has been said about Socrates referring Alcibiades to a *future instructor*, as if he had been sensible of the want of supernatural communication, and that he hoped for, and expected it. But supposing Plato's account of the conversation, (p. 295.) to be depended upon, which it certainly cannot, I can by no means infer so much from it. After expressing the uncertainty men are under with respect to proper requests to the gods, he tells Alcibiades that "he must wait till some person in-"form him (τις μαθῃ) how he should conduct "himself both with respect to the gods and to "men."

When, in reply to this, Alcibiades expresses much importunity to be informed who this teacher was, taking for granted that it was some man (for he says "I would gladly know who this man "is,") Socrates only says, that "it was one who "cared much for him," meaning probably that he was much his friend; "but that at present a degree "of darkness hung over his mind, which must "first be dispersed." I therefore think it most probable

probable that he meant *himself*, but that he thought his pupil not then sufficiently prepared to receive farther instruction on the subject.

3. We see in the case of Socrates himself, as well as in that of the people of Athens in general, the strong attachment which the heathens had to the rites of their ancient religions. To disregard them, and to adopt other rites, was punishable with death. The Athenians, as well as other nations, occasionally adopted the worship of other gods, and other gods, and other modes of worship, cut individuals were not allowed to do it. It must be done by the authority of the state, and at Athens it was by the court of Areopagus. On this account the apostle Paul, who was said to endeavour to introduce the worship of strange gods, and a new religion, was brought before this court.

But though heathen nations sometimes adopted other rites, they never abandoned their ancient ones. There does not appear to have been any example of this in all antiquity. Nor can we wonder at this, when it is considered, that in all heathen countries, the prosperity of the state was thought to depend upon the observance of the religious rites of their ancestors, the founders of the respective states. No principle appears to have been more fixed in the minds of all men than this. We see it in the extreme reluctance with which some of the most absurd and indecent rites, as the Lupercalia at Rome, were given up. And to the very last, the more learned, and therefore, it may be presumed, the least superstitious of the Romans, constantly upbraided the christians with being the cause of the decline of the empire, by the introduction of their new religion.

This attachment of the heathens to their religion was necessarily increased by its entering into all the customs, and confirmed habits, of common life; some rite of a religious nature being observed from the time of their birth to that of their death, and in fact from the morning to the evening of every day. Every entertainment, public or private, was tinctured with it. No act of magistracy could be performed without it; and in countries the most advanced in civilization the public festivals, in honour of their gods, were very numerous. It will be seen in *Potter's Antiquities of Greece*, that not less than sixty-six of them were observed by the Athenians, and several of them were of some days continuance. And in general there was so much in them of festivity and amusement, bordering, to say the least, on licentiousness, that they were very fascinating to the common people. When

When it is considered how discordant and inconsistent all this was with the principles of christianity, so that when any heathen became a christian he must change every habit of his life, as well as his opinions; that let him live ever so privately, he could hardly pass a single day without the change being observed, and that at the birth of a child, a marriage, or a funeral, it must have been conspicuous to all his neighbours, and the whole city, though he might have found some excuse for not attending the public sacrifices, and other rites of a visible nature, and though he should not have thought himself obliged (which all christians are) to make an open profession of his faith, *confessing Christ before men*, we shall not wonder at the difficulty with which this great change must have been made, any more than at the alarm that was taken when many converts were made to christianity, and the consequent persecution of christians, as seditious persons, men *who turned the world upside down*, (Acts xvii. 6.) their principles tending to the ruin of all states.

While the christians were few, and generally considered as converts to judaism, which was universally tolerated, and while they behaved in a very peaceable inoffensive manner, they might not give much alarm, notwithstanding their singularities; but when they were observed to be numerous, they would not fail to give alarm to all heathen governors. They were then exposed to the most unrelenting persecution, except where the acting magistrates were secretly disposed in their favour.

The rapid progress of christianity in these circumstances will ever appear the most extraordinary thing in the history of the world. It appears from the epistle of Paul, that in his time there were christian churches in all the more considerable cities in the eastern part of the Roman empire. In the time of the emperor Trajan, the younger Pliny, then governor of Bithynia, complained that the rites of the ancient religions were generally discontinued in his province; and in the space of about three hundred years so numerous and respectable were the christians become, in the whole extent of that vast empire, that the emperors themselves found they might safely declare themselves christians.

To account for the rise and progress of christianity, and the overthrow of heathenism, and this without violence, in the whole extent of the Roman empire, in so short a space of time, is a problem that no unbeliever has seriously attempted to

solve,

solve, except Mr. Gibbon may be said to have endeavoured to do it. But his observations on the subject are so exceedingly futile, that they discover equal prejudice and ignorance, ignorance of the common principles of human nature, of the nature of heathenism, and of the state of the heathen world. I proposed to enter into the discussion of this important subject with him, but he petulantly declined it, as may be seen in the letters that passed between us relating to it, published in the *Appendix to the first volume of my Discourses on the evidence of revealed religion*, and also in the *Life of Mr. Gibbon* by one of his friends. At my time of life I cannot engage in this, or any other controversy; but I earnestly wish, as a friend to important truth, that some learned and candid unbeliever (and such I doubt not there are) would engage in it. He would find christians enow equally learned and candid to discuss the question with him.

4. Neither Socrates nor Jesus were writers; and there seems to be more of dignity in their characters in consequence of it, as if they were not very solicious about transmitting their names to posterity; confident, that as far as it was an object with them, it would be sufficiently done by others. All the accounts, therefore, that we have of them come

from their disciples and friends. And there is a remarkable difference in the manner in which the life of Socrates is written by Xenophon, and that of Jesus by the evangelists. There cannot be a doubt but that the evangelists had a much higher opinion of their master than Xenophon or Plato had of theirs. The traces of this are numerous, and indisputable; but there is not in their writings any direct *encomium*, or *praise*, of him, as there is in the Greek writers of Socrates; and yet without any assistance of this kind a reader of moderate discernment cannot help forming a much higher idea of Jesus than he does of Socrates from the *facts* recorded of him, and the *discourses* ascribed to him.

Indeed, we have no example of such simplicity in writing as that of the scriptures of the Old and New Testaments in all the heathen world; and it is not easy to account for the difference, especially with respect to the later writers; except that Moses having begun to write in this simple manner, the succeeding writers, having no other model, naturally followed that; inserting in their compositions nothing that appeared superfluous, as direct encomiums are, when the facts from which such encomiums are drawn, are before the reader; who may be supposed as capable of drawing a proper inference from them as the writer himself. As

As the sacred writers say nothing directly in praise of those whom they most esteemed and admired, they say nothing directly in dispraise, or censure, of those whom they most disliked, but leave the circumstances they simply mention to make their natural impression upon their readers. And from the effects of these two different modes of writing, the *natural* and the *artificial*, as they may be termed, the former appears to be better calculated to answer the purpose of the writer than the latter. When a man directly praises or censures another, we suspect some previous bias for or against him, and are upon our guard; but when we read a simple narrative of facts, without any explanatory remarks of the writer; we have no suspicion of any thing unfavourable to truth. We think we see with our own eyes, and hear with our own ears, and that we thus judge for ourselves.

My father to shew how little stress he laid on a casual opinion, has directed me to add the following sentence concerning the Demon of Socrates—from his second tract in answer to Dr. Linn, and to insert it at the end of the section relating to Socrates. J. P.

As to the Demon of Socrates, on which you urge me so closely, I professed not to have any fixed opinion about it. If I had been asked what I thought of it a short time before the writing of my pamphlet, I should have said, as you do, it was probably nothing more than his own good sense, but on considering his character more particularly, I was unwilling to think that such a man would persist through life, and to his dying moments, in telling a lie. And what the Supreme Being might please to do by or with him, or any man, neither you nor I can tell. But I never said, as you now quote me, that "God spake to Socrates by a demon," which you call, (p. 75,) "a glaring deformity of my assertion. Such an idea never occurred to me. As my opinion on this very unimportant subject is unsettled, it is very possible that I may revert to my former opinion, and yours about it.

ON

ON PLATONISM.

INTRODUCTION.

PLATO was the professed disciple of Socrates, and attended him eight years. His attachment to him appears by the sum that he raised to procure his release from imprisonment, and his eagerness to speak in his defence at his trial. The veneration in which he held his memory is evident from his making him the principal speaker in many of his dialogues, and the person who delivers his own sentiments in them.

After the death of Socrates, Plato travelled in quest of knowledge, first into Italy, where he conversed with the disciples of Pythagoras, and afterwards into Egypt, where, being known to be a person of considerable distinction in his own country, he appear to have been received with great respect, and from the Eastern part of the world in which it is is said he travelled in the disguise of a merchant, he seems to have got some knowledge, directly or indirectly, of the sytem that generally prevailed there.

That he should expect to learn something in countries out of the bounds of Greece is not extraordinary, as it is acknowledged by him, that "what the Greeks knew concerning the gods, and "their worship, was derived from the Barbarians." But he says (Epinomis.) "what the Greeks learn-"ed of the Barbarians we have improved." Notwithstanding this acknowledgment, he is willing to ascribe more merit to the Greeks than to them, when he says (Ib.) that "though there is the great-"est difficulty in the invention of these things, we "hope that all the Greeks will honour the one "God in a better manner than the Barbarians, e-"specially as instructed, and warned, by the Del-"phic oracle" (Ib.) so that, in his opinion, the Greeks had divine instruction as well as human.

He farther acknowledges that, in the early ages, "the Greeks entertained very imperfect ideas of "the gods and their worship, having low ideas of "their characters, which they did well to correct. "Because in time past, he says (Ib.) our ancestors "formed wrong opinions of the gods, and their "proge-

"progenies, as if they had been animals, we "should now treat the subject differently." In this he alludes to the marriages of the gods and goddesses, and their reputed offspring, in other gods, and also in their acceding to the popular notions, adopted and embellished by the poets, which gave him such offence that we shall find he proscribed their writings, and excluded them from his commonwealth. Indeed, these notions of the vulgar were rejected by all who pretended to philosophy, or superior knowledge, in Greece, from long before the time of Socrates, as we have seen already and to the latest period of it.

Section I.

Of God and his Providence.

The being of a god, or of gods, for Plato uses both the phrases promiscuously, he generally takes for granted. Occasionally, however he introduces arguments for his opinion, especially (De Legib. lib. 10.) from the consideration of the structure of the earth, the sun, the stars, and the whole universe. "How could bodies of such magnitude," he says. (Epin.) "perform their circuits without god. I therefore

"therefore assert that god is the cause of this, and "that there cannot be any other." He also argues "from the variety of seasons, dividing time "into years and months, and also from the con"sent of all nations, Greeks and Barbarians." (De Leg. lib. 10.) But according to him, and indeed all the heathen philosophers without exception, the *matter* out of which the world was made, was not created by god, but found by him; having existed from eternity as well as himself, but in a confused disorderly state, such as was generally termed *chaos*. The being of a God, or gods, Plato thought to be so evident, that he says (Ib.) "No person persists in his disbelief of the gods "from youth to old age."

There is a great air of piety in the writings of Plato; and this, no doubt, contributed to make his philosophy so well received by the early christians. In a letter to Dion (Epist. 4.) he says, "by "the favour of the gods things go well." The same pious language occurs again in the same letter. That he preferred the term god to that of gods is evident from his letter to Dionysius, of Syracuse (Epist. 13.) in which he informs him that, in his serious letters he begins with the term *god*, but

but that in those in which he was not serious he uses the term *gods*. This, however, is no guide to us with request to his dialogues, so that we are left to distinguish his real sentiments from those speakers to whom he gives the advantage in the argument, which, however, is sufficiently apparent.

Notwithstanding Plato's great admiration of Socrates, he did not confine himself, as Socrates did, to that philosophy which is of practical use in life, tending to rectify the dispositions of men, and inciting them to such virtues as would make them useful members of society, but indulged in various speculations concerning the nature of God and the universe, and in a manner that his master would not have approved. Indeed, on these great but obscure subjects he is in many respects perfectly unintelligible.

According to Plato, the universe was constructed by the supreme being, whom he frequently distinguishes by the title of (αγαθος) without the instrumentality of any subordinate being, according to a pattern of it previously formed in his own mind. But there is great confusion in his account of these *ideas in the divine mind*, (which he, no doubt, borrowed from the Pythagoreans as was observed before) so that he sometimes makes them

a sea second principle of things, and distinguishing between what is *sensible* from what is *intellectual* in man; and considering all that we see here as the object of the *senses*, he supposes these ideas to be invisible to the senses, but comprehended by the intellect; and though they exist in the divine mind, the intellect of man has free access to them. He therefore calls them *things intelligible*, and says that what we see here are only the shadows of them, and changeable, whereas those intelligible ideas are the only things that are unchangeable, and permanent. The great object of philosophy, according to him, is to raise the mind to the contemplation of these higher, intelligible, and permanent, objects.

Aristotle ascribes this view of things to Heraclitus. "The doctrine of *ideas*, he says, is advanc-
" ed by those who were convinced by Heraclitus,
" that sensible things are always flowing, and
" changeable; so that if there be any such thing
" as *real knowledge*, which was supposed to re-
" quire a *fixed object*, there must be things of a dif-
" ferent nature from those that are the object of our
" senses. They must be fixed, there being no
" proper knowledge of things that are flowing."
(Metaph, Lib. 12. Cap. 4.)

To

To this doctrine Plato seems to allude when he says (De. Leg. Lib. 10.) "All see the body of "the sun, but not the soul that animates it; Not "being the object of any of our senses, it is seen "by the mind." All the meaning that I can make of this doctrines of ideas, perceived by the intellect, and not by the senses, things not fluctuating and variable, as the objects that we converse with are, is that they mean what we call *abstract ideas*, as those of horses, men, trees, &c. divested of the circumstances of colour, size, place, &c. which always attend individual objects; and in this there is no great mystery, but still every actual idea has some peculiarity or other, as well as real objects.

On this mysterious doctrine of ideas, which were personified by the later Platonists, and made a kind of *second god*, the immediate author of the creation, was founded the doctrine of the *christian trinity*, as I have shewn at large in my *History of Early Opinion concerning Jesus Christ.* The mischief that has arisen from false metaphysical principles has been most extensive, affecting every article of christian faith and practice, as may be seen in several of my writings. Indeed, no branch of science has wholly escaped this subtle and baleful influence. Happily, however, good sense is at length

length prevailing over every thing that is not founded on reason and truth; and with this, though seemingly foreign to the subject of religion, we are deriving that light which exhibits christianity in its best and purest state, as it came from Christ and the apostles, who knowing nothing of heathen philosophy, or metaphysics, delivered the plainest truths in the plainest language, though they have since their times been most strangely perverted by an unnatural mixture of heathen principles, and heathen superstition.

Notwithstanding the absurdity of Plato's metaphysical notions concerning the nature of God, and his relation to the universe, his ideas of his *attributes*, and of his *providence*, were in general just and excellent, agreeing with those of the scriptures.

Having frequently represented the Supreme Being as the friend of virtue, and the enemy of vice, he says, (De. Leg. Lib. 10.) "God cannot have "the disposition that he hates. God approves of "those who resemble himself, and is angry (νεμεσα) "with those who are unlike to him. But nothing "is so like God as a good man...... He is the most "sacred of all things," (Alcib. 2.) meaning that he has the nearest relation to divinity.

The

The term by which he generally characterizes the Supreme Being is in the singular number, viz. the *Good*, (ἀγαθὸς) vindicating his most essential attribute. "Evil," he says (Rep. 3.) "cannot "come from God," and in (Rep. xi.) "we must "look to some other than God for the cause of e-"vil." This principle, however, he did not carry so far as the Stoics, who maintained that God was incapable of *anger*, so that he would not punish even the wicked. On the contrary, Plato represents the Supreme Being, though termed *the Good*, as no less *just* than merciful. "That there are "gods," he says (De. Leg. Lib. 10.) "and that "they are good, and respect justice more than "men, is the best introduction to a body of laws." After denominating him, "the beginning, the mid-"dle, and the end, and the supporter of all things," he says (De. Leg. Lib. 4.) "he is always accompa-"nied by justice, and punishes those who depart "from the divine law. The humble follow him "quiet and composed, but he that is elevated by "his riches, his beauty, or any other advantage, as "if he stood in no need of a guide, is deserted by "him; and though such a person may appear en-"viable to man, in the end he destroys himself, his "family, and the state." Agreeably to this, he says, (De. Leg. Lib. 10.) "Let not the suc-"cess of wicked and unjust men, who, though not "truly happy, are generally reputed to be so, and "who are extolled in poems and discourses, drive "thee rashly into impiety; nor be disturbed tho' "they should continue so to old age, and this pros-"perity should extend to their children. Nor be "thou angry with the gods who permit this, or "think that they neglect the affairs of men; for "they will not be exempt from punishment after "death."

Veracity is another moral attribute that Plato ascribes to God. "The nature of God, and of "demons," he says, (De. Rep. Lib. 2.) "ad-"mits not of falsehood; for God is altogether "simple, and true in his words and actions. He "neither changes himself, nor can he deceive o-"thers, by vicious speeches, or omens, to men "sleeping or awake." This he says by way of censure on Homer, who represents Jupiter as acting in this deceitful and unworthy manner, disgraceful to a man, and much more so to a God. To the divine character in this respect he seems to allude, though with much obscurity, when he says, (De. Rep. Lib. 6.) "As light and our view of it, "are not the sun, but the resemblance of the sun,

"so

"so knowledge and truth are the image of *the Good*, "but not the Good," meaning God. The majesty of the Good itself is greater. Agreeably to this honourable idea of the divine character, he says that "the offerings to God," meaning those that are most acceptable to him, "are honour, venera-"tion, and gratitude," (Euthyphro.)

But notwithstanding this, we shall see that, like all the other heathen philosophers, Plato strongly recommends a conformity to the idolatrous rites of religious worship established in his country, and even the rigorous punishment of all that did not conform to them; so far were they from following the light they really had, and so little prospect was there of the world in general being enlightened, and and reformed, by their instructions.

The writings of Plato contain several just and beautiful illustrations of the providence and moral government of God. "God," he says, (Politicus) "is the shepherd of mankind, taking the same care "of us that a shepherd does of his sheep and oxen. "He takes care (De. Leg. Lib. 10.) of the smallest "things as well as of the greatest. None of the "causes of neglect in men can take place with re-"spect to God. We all acknowledge," he says,

(Ib.) "that the Gods see every thing, that they are "all powerful and good, yea the best possible, nor "can they be affected by idleness or fear. They, "therefore, cannot despise or neglect any thing be-"cause it is small. Besides, there is more diffi-"culty in seeing, and disposing of, small things "than of great ones."

"The universe," he adds, "belongs to God, "and he will not neglect what is his own. He "cannot be called a wise physician who only at-"tends to the body in general, and not to the par-"ticular parts. Nor do governors of cities, or "masters of families, neglect small things. Ar-"chitects also make use of small stones in laying "the larger ones. And let us not think that God, "who is the wisest of all, is less wise than man. "Besides man is a worshipper of the gods," and therefore more deserving of his attention and care.

To shew that the Supreme Being is incapable of being diverted from the just administration of affairs by any unworthy motive, he says (De. Leg. Lib. 10.) "To say that the gods are easily appeas-"ed, is to compare them to dogs or wolves, which "are pacified by giving them part of the plunder, "and then suffer them to worry the sheep. Cha-

"rioteers

"rioteers are not to be bribed, nor are commanders "of armies, or physicians, nor are husbandmen "or shepherds to be deceived in this manner, nor "even can crafty wolves thus deceive dogs. And "are the gods the greatest guardians of the greatest things, and are the keepers of the greatest "things worse than dogs, or men of moderate capacity, who never act unjustly deceived by the "bribes of unjust men?"

There is hardly any advantage that men are possessed of that Plato does not ascribe to the gods, and to their good will to men. "It appears to me," he says (Philebus,) "that God sent gifts to men by "Prometheus, together with fire. It is not by "art," he says, (Epin.) "but by nature, and the "favour of the gods, that we cultivate the earth." He makes God the author of friendship, by disposing dispositions that are similar, and formed for friendship, to unite. (Lysis,) "In the forming of "states," he says, (De. Leg. Lib. 4.) "we must "begin with invoking the gods, that they may be propitious to us, and assist us in making laws." And after representing the advantage of the right worship of the gods, as the most important of all things to be attended to, he says, (Epin.) "No man "can rightly teach this without the assistance of

He even ascribes to divine inspiration the great things that eminent statesmen do for their country, without understanding the nature, or foreseeing the consequences of them, adding, that "all good men "are in some sense divine." (Meno.)

It must have been among the Pythagoreans that Plato learned what he writes, but in a manner that is very unintelligible, concerning *numbers*, of which their philosophy made great use. It seems most probable that by metaphysical reasoning they made the Supreme Being to be represented by *unity*; and as all numbers consist of unity repeated, and after thus proceeding from it are resolvable into it again; so all things, after proceeding from their *first cause*, will be resolved into it. But this is not the only use that Plato, no doubt after the Pythagoreans, made of this comparison. But whatever be the knowledge that we derive from this source, Plato ascribes it to God. "We affirm," he says, (Epin.) "that numbers are the gift of God, and "on them all the arts of life depend, but this no "prophet (μαντις) can comprehend. Whate- "ver is wicked and irregular is deficient with re- "spect to number. Many animals cannot learn "from their parents the use of numbers. It is "God that gives us this power. The excellent "ancient,

" ancients," he says, (Philebus) " who were near-" er to the gods than we are, taught us that the uni-" verse consists of *one* and *many*, which always has " been, and ever will be. The resemblance of " numbers dissimilar in their nature, when reduced " to a plane, is evident; and this to a person of " understanding must appear not to be a human, " but a divine wonder" (Epin.) We do not, however, find, that this mysterious doctrine of numbers was taken up by any of the succeeding sects of philosophy, so that it probably died with Plato.

Section II.

Of the Polytheism of Plato.

With all Plato's knowledge of the divinity, of his attributes, and his universal providence, and of his preference of the term *god* to that of *gods*, when he is treating of the divine nature, he was, like all heathens, a polytheist, and like them an advocate for the strict observance of the idolatrous rites of his country.

He seems to have learned the doctrine of two principles in the East, from his sayings (De. Leg.

 Lib. 10.)

Lib. 10.) "Are there one or more souls? Not less "than two, the one beneficent, and the other ma- "leficent*;" and also from his saying, as was quoted before, that "we must look to something "else than god for the source of evil." But this was never a doctrine that prevailed in the West. But that Plato considered more beings than one to be entitled to the rank of gods, is evident from his saying (Epin.) "why should we not take the part "of god who is the author of all good. But which "of gods, perhaps *the heavens*, which we consider "as the most righteous, as all the demons and the "other gods agree to honour him; and pray to "him above all." What he meant by the divinity of the *heavens*, whether the Supreme Being, or the sun, is not clear.

He evidently considered all the celestial bodies as animated, and intitled to the rank of gods. "The "divine race of stars," he says, (Epin.) must be "considered as celestial animals, with most beau- "tiful bodies, and happy blessed souls; and that "they

* *By this he might mean* matter, *which was by some considered as refractory, and the only source of evil. But by saying it was* maleficent, *he seemed to consider it as a principle that had intelligence, and activity.*

"they have souls is evident from the regularity of "their motions." In a manner that to me is perfectly unintelligible, he derives the different orders of gods from the different elements in nature, placing them, after mentioning by name Jupiter, Juno, and the demons, according to their different ranks, and provinces (Epin.) He seems, too, to have considered the earth as a proper deity, and the parent of the animals that exist upon it. "For the same "reason" he says, (Menexenus.) "that a mother "bears her children, the earth has produced men. "For it is the earth, and nothing else, that supplies "them with food, as having itself produced them."

Plato's dread of innovations in matters of religion, appears from the following passage in his Epinomis. "A legislator of the least understanding "will make no innovations, and take care not to "turn his state to any other mode of worship, or "dare to move what his country has established by "law or custom concerning sacrifices; for he "knows that no mortal can come at any certainty "with respect to these matters." And yet he approved of such additions to the public rites as would be an improvement upon any of them. "A "legislator," he says (Ib.) "will be free from "blame if he thinks better of the gods than his "predecessors, and by excellent discipline honour "them with hymns and praises, and live according-"ly." This, however, was not introducing the worship of new gods.

Having distinguished the crime of *impiety* into three kinds, viz. the maintaining that there are no gods, that they take no care of human affairs, or that they are easily appeased by sacrifices, (De. Leg. Lib. 10.) he prescribes the following punishment for the different degrees of guilt in this respect.

"If a man neglect the gods by omitting sacrifi-"ces and despising oaths, he must be punished, "lest he make others like himself. There are ma-"ny who deceive others in this manner, deserving "to die more than one or two deaths. Others de-"serve only castigation or imprisonment. They "who think that the gods neglect human affairs, "and they who think them easily appeased, are not "to be confounded. They who think so not from "any bad principle, but a kind of madness, should "be imprisoned not less than five years, without "any citizen being allowed to go near them, except "those who will admonish them of their errors. If "after

"after this they continue in their impiety, they "must be punished with death."

"Some who are obstinate in these opinions, and "draw many after them, especially the common "people, whole families, and the state," meaning no doubt, the danger of influencing the whole state, "should be confined in prisons surrounded by the "sea, where no free person should have access to "them, and when they die, they should be buried "without the bounds of the state; and if any per-"son should bury them, he should be accounted "guilty of impiety. If he had children, they should "be taken care of by the state from the time that "the father was condemned."

"There should also be a general law to prevent "any person from making what gods, or what sa-"cred rites, he pleases; and for this reason no per-"sons should have chapels for worship in their own "houses, but perform their worship in public, and "be punished like they do so. If any person, not "from childishness, but from depraved impiety, "act in this manner, by sacrificing either in private "or in the public worship of the gods, let him be "condemned to death as impure; and let the re-"gulators of the laws judge concerning the mo-"tives of his conduct." (De. Leg. Lib. 10.)

So

So intolerant were the wisest and best disposed of all the heathens with respect to religion, that we cannot wonder at the dread they entertained of christianity, when it began to spread, as it was according to their ideas, the height of *impiety;* aiming at nothing less than the overthrow of every thing that was deemed the most sacred, and what had been established from time immemorial, and on which it was universally taken for granted that the well being of every state depended.

But Christ was fully aware of this difficulty, and he apprized his followers of it. He enabled them, however, to overcome it, though they were forwarned that they should be *hated of all men for the sake of his name*, that is, merely for being christians, and that *they who killed them would think they did God service;* which was actually the case, both with respect to Jews and heathens. And great as this obstacle was, which made all that was powerful in the world the enemy, of christianity it finally triumphed; and it is now the prevailing religion in all those countries in which Jupiter, Juno, and numberless other objects of heathen worship, were most revered, but whose names are now to be learned from history only. This is an argument of peculiar importance with respect to the evidence

of

of christianity, but can only be felt and understood by those who are acquainted with the opinions and prejudices of the heathens at the time of its promulgation. And these opinions and prejudices appear now to be so unreasonable, and extraordinary, that a faithful account of them is barely credible. That Plato was both sensible of the great ignorance of the common people on the subject of religion, and of the hazard that might be the consequence of informing them better, appears from his saying (Timæus.) " It is a difficult thing " to discover the nature of the creator of the uni- " verse, and being discovered, it is impossible, to " expose the discovery to vulgar understandings.

This intolerance in matters of religion is the more extraordinary in the case of Plato, as he acknowledges the imperfection of the popular religion when it was first instituted in Greece, and commends those statemen who improved it, in order to do more honour to their gods; and as he condemns such poems as these of Homer and Hesiod, because they led persons, and especially young persons, to entertain unworthy notions of their gods; when it must have been evident to himself, and every one else, that the popular religion, which he wished to perpetuate, was founded altogether on those very notions. Hesiod and Homer did not

make

make a religion for the Greeks, but only made use of what they found universally received to embellish their poems, and to please those before whom they were to be recited.

So much was Plato offended at these poems, and all others of the same nature and tendency, that he excluded them all, without exception, from his commonwealth, though he would retain such hymns as were composed in honour of the gods. But even the hymns, if they resembled those ascribed to Homer, or those of Callimachus, are similar to the poems of Hesiod and Homer, repeating the same popular and absurd stories. "We reject," he says (De. Rep. Lib. 2.) "poems from this "commonwealth, because they deceive men, as "Hesiod by his accounts of Cœlum and Saturn; "which, if they were true, ought to be concealed "rather than divulged. For it must not be told a "young man, that the greatest crimes may be "committed without any thing extraordinary hap-"pening, or that a man who punishes an offending "parent does no wrong, but what the greatest and "best of the gods have done. The imitation of "the poets," he says, (De. Rep. Lib. 3.) "at-"tended to in early years affects the morals and "nature itself, with respect to the body, the "speech, and the very thought." This

This is the more extraordinary in Plato, as he a-scribes to the poets a real inspiration, the same that was generally ascribed to the priestesses of Apollo at Delphi (Meno.) "Poets who" he says, "re-"semble the Corybantes, who are seized with a di-"vine afflatus, and know not what they do. They "are the interpreters of the gods." (Io.)

Section III.

Of the Human Soul.

The sentiments of Plato concerning the *human soul* are by no means clear and distinct, nor are they pursued by him to their natural consequences, as they were by the stoics afterwards.

Matter was always acknowledged to be incapable of any kind of *action*, and was always thought to be *acted upon;* whereas the igneous nature of the soul was supposed to give it natural activity. A-greeable to this, Plato says (De. Leg. Lib. 10.) "The soul has the power of moving itself."

He is not uniform in denying what was called *passion* to the mind. He must, therefore, mean it in a gross sense when he says (De. Leg. Lib. 10.) "Where there is passion, there must be generati-

"on;

"on; and this applies to the body," meaning, no doubt that where there is generation, there must be a succession of beings produced from one another, that the death of some may make room for others; whereas mind is incapable of any such thing, and consequently of that kind of passion which leads to it. It must, therefore, be immortal, and in this doctrine Plato is perfectly uniform and consistent.

"Every soul," he says (Phœdrus.) "is immortal. That which is always in motion is from "eternity, but that which is moved by another "must have an end." Accordingly he mentioned the *pre-existence*, as well as the *immortality*, of the soul; and in the East these two doctrines always went together, and are always ascribed to Pythagoras; the soul and the body being supposed to have only a temporary connection, to answer a particular purpose. "The soul existed," he says (De. Leg. Lib. 10.) "before bodies were produc- "ed, and it is the chief agent in the changes and "the ornament of the body."

Agreeably to this doctrine of pre-existence, Plato maintained that all the knowledge we seem to acquire here is only the recollection of what we

knew

knew in a former state. "It behoves man," he says (Phœdrus.) "to understand how many sensati-"ons are united in one, and this is the recollection "of what the soul, when in a state of perfection "with God, saw before."

So greatly superior, in the idea of all the heathen philosophers, was the soul to the body, the latter being intirely subservient to the former, that we cannot wonder that they consider the soul as the whole *self* of a man, and the body as a thing foreign to him. "The mind," Plato says, (De. Leg. Lib. 12.) "is all that we call *ourselves*, and the body "attends it: meaning as a servant. It is only af-"ter death," he says (De. Rep. Lib. 10.) "when it "has got rid of the clog of the body, that we can "see what the soul really is;...... whether com-"pound or simple, and the whole of its condition." It is on this supposition of the independence of the mind on the body, that he advances one of his arguments for the immortality of the soul. "The "soul," he says, (Ib.) "cannot die by any affecti-"of the body, but only by some disorder peculiar "to itself. The soul by the death of the body "does not become more unjust, and the death of "the body is not the punishment of its injustice, "but other punishments. For death is to it a free-

"dom from every evil. Since, then, neither the "death of the body, nor its own depravity, can "destroy the soul, it must be immortal."

That the souls of men are emanations from the Supreme Being, the fountain of all intelligence, seems to have been taken for granted by Plato, but I do not find it distinctly expressed in any part of his writings. He seems, however, to allude to it in a passage that I quoted before. But he generally considers it as retaining its individuality after death; as when he says (De. Leg. Lib. 12.) "In "truth the soul of each of us is immortal, and "goes to the other gods, to give an account of its "actions." This agrees with his uniform language about the rewards of virtue, and the punishments of vice, after death. Whether souls are to be reunited to their source afterwards, which he probably supposed, as being held to be the necessary consequence of their being originally derived from it, this retribution he must have thought would previously take place.

With respect to the *threefold division of man*, a doctrine held by later philosophers, I do not find any thing clear, or consistent, in Plato. And the term (ψυχη) which in other writers signifies the mere *animal principle* in man of which they partake

in

common with the brutes, he applies to the highest principle, that of *intelligence in* him, when he says (Alcib. 1.) " The body is not the man, but the soul (ψυχη) which makes use of, and commands, the body."

SECTION IV.

Of Virtues and Vices.

On the subject of *virtue and vice* it may be taken for granted that the sentiments of Plato were not, in general, different from those of Socrates; so that it is unnecessary to make quotations from his writings recommending the practice of virtue, and dissuading from that of vice. His belief in the being and providence of God, and in a future state of retribution, must have laid a foundation for piety, and the practice of virtue in general, if what he advances on those subjects were his real sentiments; and the frequency with which he urges them, and the stress that he lays upon them, makes it difficult to believe that they were not.

In these respects he comes nearer to the doctrines of revelation than any other of the heathen philosophers that came after him, even than Socrates himself. But his arguments in proof of the immortal-

 ity

ity of the soul, and also those for a future state, are so weak, and they made so little impression on those that came after him, that it is barely possible that he could have been influenced by them himself; and his writings in general have much the air of being calculated to please the generality of his countrymen, with whom those opinions were in some sense popular, and to whom they would, of course, tend to recommend him. And it is evident from his history that he was much more desirous of general applause than his master. On this account there will always remain some doubt with respect to the real sentiments of Plato on these important subjects. Judging of him by his writings, we cannot wonder that his philosophy was held in such high estimation by many of the more learned of the early christians, and that they embraced it in preference to any other.

With respect to the proper objects of men's pursuits in life, Plato says (Philebus) that "neither pleasure, nor wisdom, are to be ranked with things that are absolutely *good*, because what is good is perfect, and sufficient of itself," which, he observes will not apply to either of them. But he was far from entertaining the extravagant opinion of the Stoics, in classing both pleasure and pain among

mong the things that are absolutely indifferent, unworthy of the attention of a wise man, and incapable of affecting him.

There are three remarkable exceptions to the moral maxims of Plato, in which he would not have had the concurrence of Socrates, viz. his recommending a community of women in his commonwealth, his approbation of perjury in matters of love, and in the licentiousness which he would allow soldiers on a military expedition.

How little must Plato have known of human nature, and human life, when he recommended a community of women in his republic (De. Rep. Lib. 5.) and an education of them the same with men and together with them, even so far as to exercise in the gymnasia naked; saying that nothing that was useful ought to be deemed shameful, that in former times it was thought shameful for men to exercise naked, but that now it was no longer so. Being naturally capable of doing many of the duties of men, such as serving their country both in the army and in civil offices, they ought, he says to receive an education proper to qualify them for those, though they should be exempted from what was most laborious in any of those offices. By this means, and sexual commerce being confined to a proper age, which he makes to be thirty for for men, and twenty for women, a more hardy race of men he says, would be produced.

These healthy women being accessible to more men, he says, would have more children, though this now appears to be, by a wise providence, contrary to fact, as prostitutes have seldom any children at all. The children thus promiscuously produced he would have nursed and educated together, the stronger, however, in one place, and the weaker in another by women engaged by the state for that purpose, without giving them any intimation concerning their parents. He would not, however, allow of any sexual intercourse between men and their own mothers or daughters, &c. But it is not necessary to follow him through all the details of so visionary and absurd a scheme.

Indeed, the objections to this scheme are so obvious, and so numerous, that it is not worth while to enter into any serious discussion of it. I would only observe that if frequent divorces have been found, as is universally acknowledged, to be attended with much evil, a community of women, which it has always been the very first step of civilization to prevent, must be attended with infinitely more, and greater.

With

With how much more wisdom did our Saviour forbid even divorces except on account of adultery. When the change of a partner for life is considered as *impossible*, the most discordant minds reconcile themselves to it, and live together more happily than if they had the liberty to separate, which, in that case, they would upon every trifling disgust be thinking of, and contriving; and this being the case of a whole society, jealousy, and violence in every form, would be unavoidable.

Besides, no mode of education is equal to that which arises from the affection of parents to their own children, and the attachment of children to their parents. This is a source of the purest satisfaction to both, and to the very close of life. And what has any parent to look to in the infirmities of old age comparable to the affection and attention that he may reasonably expect from his own children? What a miserable legislator must that be, who would deprive mankind of the purest source of domestic happiness for any advantage of a political nature? Besides, what is the great object of all true policy; but to give men the secure possession of their private rights, and individual enjoyments?

The second great objection to the moral maxims of Plato is his allowing of perjury in matters of love. "The laws of God," he says, (Convivium.) "allow of oaths," meaning a breach of oaths, "in "affairs of love. God," he says, (Hippias Major.) "pardons those who perjure themselves with re- "spect to love, as if they were children, and did "not know what they did." It appears too that the laws of Athens took no cognizance of these oaths. But the law of God, in our scriptures, makes no such distinction. It requires the strict- est performance of every oath.

Plato in his books on the Republic, censures with much severity the vice of Sodomy, which was too generally practiced in Greece. "We must ab- "stain," he says, (De. Leg. Lib. 8.) "from all "commerce with males. For this is being worse "than birds and beasts, among which the males "have no commerce with other males, but with "females only; and if it be not concealed from "both men and women, the criminal may be pu- "nished by deprivation of all civil offices, and be "treated like a foreigner." This, however, is prescribing a very mild and inadequate punishment for the most abominable of crimes.

Notwithstanding, this he says, (De. Rep. Lib. 5.)

5.) that "on an expedition soldiers should be allowed unbounded licence both with respect to "women and boys, as by this means they will be "more inflamed to gain the victory," meaning that with the expectation of this indulgence they will be more ready to enlist, and to engage in any hazardous enterprize.

The laws of Moses and of God relating to war are very different from this. According to them, wherever men are, in peace or in war, the same rules of morality are binding upon them, and the same punishment awaits the infringment of them.

SECTION V.

Of Death, and the Consequence of it.

In what Plato says on the subject of death, and the consequence of it, we see the stress that he laid on the practice of Virtue in general, though without distinguishing particular virtues or vices; and if he may be understood literally, his sentiments are decidedly in favour of a future state of retribution, in which individuals will retain their separate consciousness, at least till their proper rewards or punishments are completed. But much of what he advances on this subject has such a mixture of imagination, and of popular notions, that many persons entertain doubts of his writing what he really thought.

"It is impossible," he says, (Epin.) "that there "should be much happiness in this life; but there "is great hope that after death every person may "obtain the things that he most wishes for. Nor "is this new, but known both to the Greeks and "Barbarians." This is the only passage that I have found in the writings of Plato in which he lays any stress on the argument from general consent, or tradition, in favour of the reality of a future state; and here he intimates some degree of doubt, by only saying that there is *great hope* with respect to it. In other places he expresses more.

"In truth," he says, (De. Leg. Lib. 12.) "the "soul of each of us is immortal, and goes to other "gods, to give an account of its actions, as the laws "of our country express; which gives the greatest "confidence to good men, and terror to the wick-"ed, lest they should suffer the greatest punish-"ments after death for the crimes committed in "this life. A happy man," he says, (Epin.) "will "learn all that he can from nature, persuaded that "thus he will live most happily, and when he dies

"he

"he will go to a place suited to his virtue; and being thus truly initiated, and having acquired true wisdom, will pass the rest of his life in the contemplation of the most beautiful objects. Justice is the best reward of the soul, and we should not envy it those rewards of justice and universal virtue, which God has prepared for it in this life, or the next." "The gods," he adds, "must know who are just, and who are unjust, and must love the one and hate the other, and they will give to their friends every good that is in their power." (De. Rep. Lib. 10.)

Plato introduces one of his speakers in (De. Leg. Lib. 10.) addressing a young man licentiously disposed in the following manner. "O young man, who think that you are overlooked by the gods, consider that there is a seat of justice with the gods who dwell in heaven, that they who are wicked may join the wicked, and they who are good may join the good, in life and in death, and do and suffer what others like them do and suffer. Neither, therefore, do you, or any other person, presume that you will be happy, so as to escape, or brave the justice, of God. You are not overlooked by him, though you should go to the bottom of the earth, or ascend into the heavens,

"vens, but shall suffer according to your deserts, "whether here, in the infernal regions, or in some "distant place." This, however, being the address of an old citizen to a young one, may be nothing more than popular language, calculated to reclaim him from his vices, which would be injurious to the state; using such arguments, as whether thought to have any weight by the speaker or not, might make some impression on the hearer.

The state of those who die in battle, in the service of their country, Plato gives on the authority of Hesiod; saying, (De. Rep. Lib. 5.) "If Hesiod may be believed, they become terrestrial demons, expellers of evil, and the guardians of "mankind." For this, therefore, he does not make himself responsible.

In his Phœdrus Plato gives such an account of the state of souls after death, with the various periods of their purifications and transmigrations, as it is possible he might have heard in the East, but such as it was impossible he could be in earnest in professing his belief of.

"Souls do not," he says, "return to the source "from which they came in less than ten thousand "years. For they do not recover their wings till "that

"that time, except the souls of those who truly "philosophize, and who love boys," (meaning probably sensual pleasure in general) "and wis- "dom at the same time. These perform it in the "third circuit of a thousand years; if after this "they three times chuse this life, thus recovering "their wings after three thousand years. But other "souls are judged after the first term of life, some "of them going to a place of judgment under the "earth, to suffer according to their deserts, others "ascending to a place in the heavens suited to their "merit when they were in the form of men. These, "after a thousand years take their choice again, "some the life of a brute, and again that of man, "provided it had formerly been the soul of a man. "For souls that have not seen truth cannot assume "that form." This particular period of three thousand years Herodotus had from the priests of Egypt, who said that "when the soul had gone "through bodies of every kind, terrestial, ma- "rine, and also those of birds, it entered again into "that of a man, and that this was accomplished in "the space of three thousand years. This ac- "count," he adds, "some Greeks, whose names "he forebore to mention, claim as their own." (Lib. 2. ch. 123. Euterpe.)

Still

Still less can we think Plato to have given any credit to the following very absurd relation, which, however, he recites at full length (De. Rep. Lib. 10.) and without intimating any doubt of its truth. It is the story of one Eris, of Armenia, who after having lain dead on the field of battle twelve days, came to life, and then related what he said he had seen in the infernal regions, the whole agreeable to the fables of the poets, with many absurd additions; as that of the souls of particular persons chusing to pass into the bodies of different animals, that of Ajax into a lion, that of Orpheus into a swan, from his hatred of women, that of Thamyris into a nightingale, and that of Agammemnon into an eagle, &c. &c.

As Plato's account of a future state has such a mixture of fancy and fable, and so little support from *argument*, his declaration of his belief of it will admit of much doubt, as well as what he says of the immortality of the soul in general. They were Eastern doctrines, to this day firmly believed by the Hindoos and others, though Plato gives no intimation whence he had them. But excepting this doubtful case of Plato himself, they never gained any degree of credit in the West.

How happy, then, should we think ourselves, and

and how thankful to God, for the glorious light of the gospel, which leaves us under no doubt or uncertainty with respect to a future life in general, or the different conditions of the righteous and the wicked in it; and especially for that most satisfactory evidence of it in the death and resurrection of Jesus, as furnishing at the same time a *proof*, and also a *pattern* of a future universal resurrection; when *all that are in the graves shall hear the voice of the son of man and come forth, some to the resurrection of life, and others to that of condemnation*; and when *all men shall receive according to their works*. What weight has the mere opinion of Plato, or that of any heathen philosophers, admitting them to have been ever so much in earnest, compared to this?

We find nothing in our scriptures concerning the fanciful doctrine of *pre-existence*, or of the state of souls separate from the body; but are assured that as *the man* dies, the whole man shall rise again, with a perfect recollection of all that he had done, and therefore satisfied with respect to the state to which he will be sentenced corresponding to it. And this is all that we are at present concerned to know. It follows from this that we shall know our friends as well as ourselves. Jesus assured his

his apostles, that then *they should be with him wherever he should be*, and *see and partake of his glory*, and that this will also be shared *by all who believe on him through their word*, that is all sincere christians to the end of the world. We are also assured that all those who shall *suffer with* him shall also *reign with him for ever*. What ample encouragement is this to a life of virtue, and how will it enable us to bear all the troubles of this life, and the pains of death, be they what they may, with such an expectation. This is such *hope and joy set before us*, as was set before Jesus himself, and by which he was enabled to bear his cross, and to make no account of the shame of that ignominious, as well as painful, death.

OF

OF

THE PHILOSOPHY

of

ARISTOTLE.

INTRODUCTION.

ARISTOTLE was the disciple of Plato, but he appears to have been greatly superior to him, and indeed to all the other Grecian philosophers, in genius and good sense. He had also considerable advantage from having been tutor to Alexander the Great, and from being assisted by him in the study of nature, which was wholly neglected by all the other philosophers; as they confined themselves to subjects of mere speculation, which requires little or no knowledge of external things.

Aristotle, however, himself followed them too closely in their own track; and he seems to have taken great pleasure in collecting, and confuting, all their sentiments; in so much that, if he could be depended upon, it would be easy to ascertain the opinions of all the philosophers who had preceded him. But he is said to have greatly misrepresented them, in order to make it the more easy for him to expose and confute them, which it is evident he took much pleasure in doing, that his own opinions might appear the more original and respectable. Never perhaps, was so much genius employed on more useless subjects than in all that we see in the greater part of the writings of Aristotle. The works of Thomas Aquinas, and the christian schoolmen, are, in this respect, far inferior to his; but the subjects are much more important, and the trifling, as well as the subtlety, less.

Though the reading of the disquisitions of Aristotle on theological and metaphysical subjects be unspeakably tiresome, so that, probably, no person in this age, who has any proper idea of the value of his time, will ever read a tenth part of them; many of his conclusions, and summaries, are clear and striking; far more so than those of Plato, without affecting his sublimity, the art of his dialogues, or the elegance of his style; his aim seeming to have been nothing more than to express his own ideas, such as they were, in the most intelligible language. At least, so it appears to me, notwithstanding his acknowledging to Alexander, that though

though he had published his opinions, they were in fact not published, as only those who had been particularly instructed by him could understand them.

This may be true with respect to some of his writings, but it certainly is not so with respect to the generality of them; and of this the extracts that I shall make from many of them will enable the reader to judge for himself, in what he writes concerning the Supreme Being, the human soul, and the nature of virtue and vice; which are all that, in this work, I propose to consider; as nothing else in the writings of the heathen philosophers is of such a nature as that it can be brought into comparison with the doctrine of our scriptures; since the bulk of their writings relate to subjects which probably never entered the thoughts of any of the sacred writers, and indeed were the least important in themselves, being frivolous in the extreme.

It has been usual to class Aristotle among *Atheists*, and his writings, as translated and commented upon by Averroes, in a later period, were the great source of modern atheism and infidelity; but I do not see any pretence for this charge in the writings of Aristotle himself. For in them the Being and general providence of God are more distinctly asserted than in the writings of Plato; and what is particularly remarkable is, that, whereas Plato uses the term *God* and *gods* promiscuously, the latter never, I believe, occurs in any of the works of Aristotle, except once in his treatise on riches and vices, in which he evidently alludes to the popular religion. In all his serious writings he uses the term *god* (θεὸς) and never any other that implies plurality. And yet in this he was not followed by the stoics, or any other philosophers. If he was an atheist, he must not only have concealed, but have denied, and confuted, his own opinions in many parts of his writings, when he had not the least occasion to do it, as they are not calculated, as those of Plato evidently were, for the generality of readers. They are also written in such a manner as not to be at all inviting to readers in general, independently of the extreme abstruseness of the subject; so that they could only have been read by persons well versed in the philosophy of the times. Besides, it is of more importance to my object to ascertain what were the opinions of the readers, than those of the writers; and those are most likely to be found in such of their works as were calculated for general use. To my object the private senti-

sentiments of any particular man, and such as he did not think proper to divulge, or explain, are of no consequence whatever. I want to ascertain the opinions of the disciples, and of the sect in general.

Section I.

Of the Being, the Attributes, and the Providence, of God.

The reader, I am confident, will be surprised, as well as pleased, with many passages in the various writings of Aristotle, expressing his opinions concerning the nature, the attributes, and the providence of God. "God," he says, (De Mundo. cap. 6.) "is the most powerful Being, immortal, "and of perfect virtue, and though by nature in-"visible to all perishable things, he is seen in his "works, as in the air, in the earth, and in the wa-"ter, for whatever is done in them is the work of "God."

He expresses his approbation (Met. Lib. xii. cap. 7.) of those who say, that "God is from eterni-"ty, and the best of Beings, and that life, and a "continuance of existence, is in him." So far was Aristotle from representing God as of the same rank and nature with the heavenly bodies, or from giving any portion of divinity to them, that he says, (De. Mundo. cap. 6.) "God conducts the stars "according to number," that is, with regularity, "and that on this account he may be called their "Coryphœus."

Aristotle was even a professed advocate for the unity of God, and as I have observed before, he never, in expressing his own sentiments, uses the term *gods*, but always that of *God*. "There is," he says, (De Mundo. cap. 7.) "but one God, "though he has obtained many names, according "to his different attributes. By the appellations of "(Ζηv) and (Δια) united is signified that in him we live. He is Saturn, and Chronos, as having existed from eternity. "He is also called the "thunderer, the giver of rain, &c. It can only be "God that is to be understood in the Orphic "hymns. He is also called Fate, from things pro- "ceeding in a connected series; and Nemesis, as "possessed of a divine power, which he exercises "as he pleases; Adrastias, as the cause of every "thing in nature, which no person can deceive or "avoid; and Æsas, because he exists always. "What is said of the Parcæ must be explained "in the same manner. Finally, God, holding the "begin-

"beginning, the middle, and the end of all things, "operates according to nature, accompanied by "justice, called (Δικη) the vindicator of the di-"vine law when it is violated. And he who would "obtain a happy life must be a partaker of divinity "from the beginning;" meaning, that he must derive it from God.

The popular opinion of a multiplicity of gods, Aristotle explains in the following manner, (Met. Lib. xii. cap. 8.) "The heavens (ουρανος) are one, "but it has been handed down to us by our ances-"tors, and the antients, and left in the form of fi-"gure to posterity, that these are *gods*, and that e-"very part of nature has divinity in it. Other "things too of a fabulous nature are told to the "multitude, to induce them to obey the laws. For "they say that the gods are in the form of men, "and of other animals," &c.

Aristotle's doctrine concerning the providence of God he introduces by an account of an old traditi-on, which he says prevailed among their ancestors and all men, that "every thing was made by God "and out of God." He adds, as from the same tradition, which is better founded, that "nothing "can be well or safely conducted, without his care "and providence," (De Mundo. cap. 6.)

His account of the relation that God bears to the world, as its supreme governor, is peculiarly striking; considering the little light the heathens had on this most important subject. "What the pilot is "in a ship," he says, (De. Mundo. cap. 6.) "What "the charioteer is in his chariot, what the precen-"tor is in a chorus, what the law is in a state, or a "general in his army, God is in the world. What "manifold labour, motion, and care, would there "be without this." "Whereas with him every "thing succeeds without labour, without trouble, "or infirmity of body. For, being situated in a "steady and immoveable situation, every thing is "moved at his pleasure, according to the different "forms and natures of things. In this he resem-"bles the law in a state, which, being immoveable, "governs every thing in the state, all the magis-"trates having their proper place and province un-"der it. But he is greatly superior to, and more "stable than, our laws. For by him the whole "world of heaven is administered and governed. "All animals obey his laws, and even reptiles that "feed upon the earth."

It will be seen in the following passage that Aristotle had not the same, or equally just, ideas of the operations and providence of God that we are taught in in our scriptures. "God," he says, (De. Mundo. cap. 6.) "is the preserver of every thing that is "done in the world, and also the author of it, with- "out being affected by weariness, as a human "workman, or an animal, and of things at a dis- "tance, as well as near. For having his seat in "the highest region, from which he is called the "supreme (Ὕπατος) those bodies which are nearest "to him feel the most of his power; but I cannot "think him concerned in things that are low and "mean; but that rather, like the king of Persia, "he knows and acts by his agents. Thus he moves "the sun, and moon, and the whole heavens, and "is the author of every thing that is safe and saluta- "ry in the world. Not that he stands in need of "the assistance of others, as he does every thing "without difficulty, with a simple motion." (De Mundo. cap. 6.)

I would observe on this, that philosophy, as well as true piety, considers every thing in the universe as, in a proper sense, *equal* in the eye of God, who made the smallest things as well as the greatest, as equally subservient to his purpose. Moses represents him as having made by the exertion of the same power, reptiles as well as men, the grass of the field, as well as the largest trees, and all these as well as the sun, moon, and stars. "He said, let "them be, and they rose into existence." David represents all animals, as well as men, as equally dependent upon God, even for their daily food; when he says *the lions roar over their prey, and seek their meat from God; that he feedeth the ravens, when they cry, and that all creatures have their eyes up unto him, and he satisfies the desire of every living thing.* Agreeably to this, Jesus says *a sparrow falls not to the ground without him*, and it is he that so beautifully clothes the lillies of the field.

So incomprehensible has the doctrine of the universal presence, and constant agency, of *one mind* been thought by the generality of mankind, who are apt to judge of all intellects by their own, that many of the most intelligent and speculative of men have thought it necessary to provide him with some assistant, or assistants, in his extensive and various operations. Hence the origin of idolatry in general, from its being thought absolutely impossible that one mind should comprehend, and attend to, every thing. Hence the ideas of Plato were improved into the notion of *a second God*, the (Δημιουργος) or immediate agent in the work of creation; and hence also the christian *logos*, as a Being separate from the deity; and the still prevailing opinion,

opinion, that it was not God the Father, but Christ, who made the world, and the universe in general. Aristotle, therefore, must be excused in adopting this idea, as he was not singular in it. It also appeared to many others, as well as to him, that it was more *honourable* to the Supreme Being to suppose him not to be immediately concerned in any thing, that is low or mean.

Even some christian philosophers seem still to be intangled in this idea, when they speak of the operation of *general laws*, as if they could relieve the deity from any part of his immediate agency. For what are laws, or general rules, in the hands of those who have no power to execute them? Why should a stone, for example, move towards the earth? It is said, by the law of gravity. But what is that law, or any other law of nature, without a power of agency? There must, therefore, be an universal agency of the author of nature through the whole extent of his works, the meanest, as they appear to us, as well as the greatest. And what we call general laws cannot be any thing else than his general mode of acting, or exerting his power and influence. Incomprehensible as this must ever appear to us, it is not the only circumstance relating to the Supreme Being that is so. In fact, all his attri-

butse,

butes, and especially his eternal and necessary existence must ever be so to finite minds, that is, to all Beings except to himself.

There is another work ascribed to Aristotle, not now extant in Greek, but said to have been translated from the Greek into Arabic, and then from the Arabic into the Latin, in which we now have it; purporting to contain the doctrine of the Egyptians concerning God and nature, which I have not yet quoted; De secretiore parte divinæ sapentiæ secundum Ægyptios. (Lib. 14.) Indeed, it appears highly improbable that Aristotle should have written the whole of it, though the minuteness and subtlety of the discussions contained in it very much resemble his usual manner of writing.

Some of the sentiments in this work could not have been either those of Aristotle, or of any sect of philosophers, Ægyptian or others, that existed in his time, especially what he says concerning the *word of God*. "The express word of God," (Lib. x. cap 19.) "is the cause of all causes, and such "was the opinion of the Babylonians." "Again, "the true, word of divine wisdom (Lib. xiv. cap. "12.) is the most powerful of all. Who then can "comprehend its majesty and power? It is as that "of

" of a prince. In this word every thing is to be " seen, and from this all power of procreation " flows."

There are, however, two passages in this work, which, as being sufficiently agreeable to the sentiments of Aristotle quoted above, may deserve to be recited. " God," he says (Lib. iii. cap. 3.) " knows all things, past, present, and to come, as " their maker and governor, himself remaining " without motion." This, however, is not perfectly agreeable to the sentiments of Aristotle, as we have seen. The next passage is not consistent with itself, as it represents the Divine Being as having produced every thing first without any instrumentality of other beings and then with it.

" The Supreme Creator (Artifex) imitates no " created being, but produces forms inimitable by " any. Nor does he make use of any instrument " in this, but performs every thing by his own " power. God, therefore, whose name be exalted, produced the universe without any consultation, or wandering of thought. He first produced an only substance, viz. the *acting intellect*, " which he adorned with light most bright, and " most excellent of all created things, and by this " intermediate Being the highest orb was produced,

" which

"which contains intelligence and souls. By the "same are changes made in the lower world." (Lib. xiv. cap. 15.) The clause, *whose name be praised*, introduced after the mention of that of *God*, is evidently not heathen, but the language of a Jew, or a Mahometan.

Notwithstanding the justness of Aristotle's sentiments in general, concerning the being, and especially of the providence, of God, he was so entangled by his metaphysical maxims, that he did not make him the *first mover* in the universe; but assigned this province, seemingly the most important of all, to something independent of him; but to this first mover he never attributes any proper intelligence. "The first mover," he says, (Phys. Lib. viii. cap. 10.) "itself simple, and immoveable, but moving other bodies in infinite time, has "neither parts nor magnitude; since nothing finite "can have moved in infinite time, and magnitude "cannot be infinite." To support this, he maintains at large (De Anima. Lib. i. cap. 3.) that it is not necessary that that which is the mover should itself have any motion. "By a simple nod of the "first mover," he says (De Cœlo. Lib. i. cap. 2.) "all compound substances are moved, being their "superior and master."

But

But it is surely difficult to form any idea of a being, or substance, at the same time without magnitude, and without motion, and also without intelligence, whatever he meant by the *nod* abovementioned; for this he gives exclusively to God, who, according to him, was active from all eternity. Being, however, satisfied that something must have existed from eternity, and that whatever was moved must have had both a mover, and a beginning of motion, he was necessarily led to think that the first Being must have been immoveable; and as he must have been from eternity, he must, according to the other of his metaphysical maxims, have been without magnitude, which he says is necessarily finite. But these were only metaphysical and vague notions, which do not appear to have materially affected his general ideas concerning the being of God, his attributes, or his providence, on which he enlarges greatly, and seemingly with much satisfaction.

Section II.

Of the human Soul.

Though Aristotle writes very largely concerning the soul, and, according to his custom, proposes and answers a variety of subtle questions relating to it, his sentiments on the subject are by no means evident, except that they are different from those of Plato, who preceded him, and those of the Stoics who came after him. Indeed, on all subjects he seems to have taken pleasure in differing from all others, and appearing as the author of a system of his own.

Though Aristotle did not, with many other philosophers, consider the soul as the whole of *a man's self* he acknowledged it to be the principal part of a man. (αρχη) "It is so," he says (De Anima. Lib. i. cap. 1.) "of all animals. The intellect "(Ib. Lib. iii. cap. 4.) is immiscible with the body, "but the latter has its senses, as the instruments of it." He did not think so meanly of the body as not to be of opinion that it had some properties in com-

mon

mon with the soul. "The soul," he says (De Anima. Lib. i. cap. 1.) "has all its affection in "common with the body, as anger, gentleness, "compassion, confidence, joy, hatred, and lastly "love; because in all these cases the body suffers "as well as the mind."

The motion of the intellect is always *said* to consist in *thinking*, so that when this operation ceases the soul ceases to exist. He, therefore says, (Ægypt. Lib. viii. cap. 4.) "the intellect is al-"ways in motion, and an equable one."

According to a metaphysical distinction of Aristotle, and I believe peculiar to him, every substance consists of *matter* and *form*. "What then," says he "is the essence of the soul" (Ægypt. Lib. xii. cap. 13.) "If it is said to be *form*, it is said wisely "and rationally, being part of the compound, and "not the whole." These two last quotations are from that work of Aristotle which I have observed to be of doubtful authority. I find, however, a better (though the account is not so clear) in his (De Anima. Lib. iii. cap. 4.) where he says, "They think justly who are of opinion that the "soul is to be classed with forms. It is not, howe-"ver, wholly place, but intellectual, nor does it con-"sist in *act*, but in the *power of the forms*." This last expression is to me wholly unintelligible. But the opinion that the soul is the form of the body, whatever was really meant by it, was the common language first of the christian Aristotelians, and then of unbelievers, on the revival of the Aristotelian philosophy in the West. It was condemned at the twelfth council of Lateran.

Like all other philosophers, Aristotle considered the soul as consisting of different parts, each having its peculiar functions. "Nothing," he says (De Anima. Lib. ii. cap. 2.) "is very clear concerning "the intellectual or contemplative part of the soul; "but it seems to be another kind of soul, and that "this is separable" (meaning from its other faculties) "immortal, and incorruptible. The soul" he says, "is divisible (Mag. Mor. Lib. i. cap. 5.) "into two parts, that which has reason, and that "which is without reason, (which he must have "learned from the Pythagoreans.) In the part which "has reason, are the virtues of prudence, wisdom, "genius, memory, &c. but in the part which has not "reason, temperance, fortitude, justice, and whatever else is praise worthy in the class of virtues; "since on account of these we are deemed worthy of "praise." Here he gives to a part of the soul the same properties that other philosophers more generally

rally give to the animal part of man, of which, however, he makes no distinct mention, though he does of another part, which he calls *vegetative*, not acknowledged by any others; who in their definitions of man never descend lower than the principle of animal nature. "A part of the soul," he says (De Anima. Lib. ii. cap. 2.) "we call vegative, "of which plants partake, for the soul is (αρχη) "the principle of all vegetative, sensation intellect "and motion."

What Aristotle is represented as saying in the doubtful treatise mentioned before, favours the idea which prevailed at the revival of his philosophy, of *a common principle of life and motion*, tho' not directly, of *intelligence*, pervading all nature, and resolvable into its source at the death of each individual. "Plants and animals," he says (Ægypt. Lib. viii. cap. 2.) "besides that soul which is pe-"culiar to each, enjoy the life of the common soul; "because they cannot give aliment to others with-"out parting with their own lives. The first au-"thor of form," he says (Ib.) "gave reason to the "common soul." He even says that this is the *principle of life*, though he does not call it a *soul*. It is in all the elements, "in fire, air, and water." Here however he allows a separate individual soul to each, besides a participation in the common soul.

The doctrine of the *pre-existence of souls* and of their descent into mortal bodies, I do not find mentioned in any of the genuine writings of Aristotle; but it is mentioned in the doubtful treatise quoted above, in the exordium to which he says (Ægypt, Lib. i. cap. 1.) "We shall then describe the de-"scent of souls into bodies, and their ascent." But I do not find that he does this in any part of this treatise.

Concerning the state of the soul, or of the man, after death, Aristotle is nearly silent; and what he does say, or rather hint, is expressive of much doubt. "If any thing," he says (De Moribus. Lib. i. cap. 11.) "be enjoyed by the dead, whether "good or evil, it must be very little, either in it-"self, or to them; not sufficient to make them "happy or unhappy, who were not so before." This with respect to the souls, or the shades, of the virtuous, is pretty nearly the sentiment which Homer puts into the mouth of Achilles in the Elysian fields; who says, he had rather be a slave to the meanest person upon earth, than king of all in the regions below.

SECTION

Section III.

Of Happiness, and of Virtue and Vice.

Aristotle's ideas of happiness, and of things that should be classed among *goods* or *evils*, are very different from those of the Stoics who came after him, and, as may be inferred from what he says, those of many who preceded him; but they are far more agreeable to reason and the common sense of mankind.

In consequence of his making more account of the body than other philosopers of his time did, he justly observes (De Moribus. Lib. i. cap 4.) that "if good be *one*, which he says is the common opi-"nion, or a thing separate from every other, and in-"dependent of every other, it cannot be procured "by man, or depend upon any actions of his. "Some kinds of good," he says, (Mag. Mor. Lib. i. cap. 3.) "relate to the soul, and the virtues, and "some to the body, as health, beauty, and other ex-"ternal things, opulence, &c. It is agreed by "all," he says, (Eudem. Lib. vi. cap. 13.) "that "grief (λυπη) is an evil, and to be avoided. For "whatever is to be avoided is an evil, and whatever "is to be pursued is a good. It is not easy" he farther says, "for him to be completely happy, who "is either remarkably deformed, or of mean condi-"tion, or who lives a solitary life, or is without "children; and much less if he have children that "are very profligate. Some, therefore, place hap-"piness in outward prosperity, and some in virtue. "He, therefore, must be pronounced happy, who "is both virtuous, and possessed of external "goods." (De Moribus. Lib. i. cap. 9 and cap. 11.) In this opinion he would now, I believe, have the general concurrence of mankind.

On the subject of *virtues and vices*, the ideas of Aristotle are peculiar to himself, but he was certainly at liberty to make his own definitions, though this may lead to mistake when they are different from those that are commonly received.

Now virtue is, I believe, universally considered as the property of the soul, independent of any thing relating to the body, and only on the will and intention, arising from the inward disposition of the mind. But it is not so with Aristotle. He considers every circumstance that is *reputable*, and that makes a man appear to advantage in the eyes of others, as a virtue, (αρετη) and every thing that is disreputable, as a vice. His general definition (De Virtutibus.)

Virtutibus.) is that whatever is commendable is virtuous, and vice the contrary.

Thus, under the head of liberality, besides what we call *generosity*, he includes "neatness in dress, "elegance in a house," and this, he says, "without any regard to utility. He also is to be classed "among the liberal who keeps animals for pleasure, "or for the sake of being admired."

After mentioning Plato's division of the soul into three parts, he assigns the virtues peculiar to each of them. "Of the *rational* part of man," he says, "the virtue is prudence, of the animal "(θυμοειδους) the virtues are gentleness, and fortitude; of the concupiscible part, (επιθυμητικου) "the virtues of temperance and continence; and "those of the whole soul are justice, liberality, and "magnanimity." (De Virtutibus et Vitiis.) I do not, however, find the above mentioned division of the faculties of the soul in the works of Plato.

Aristotle's ideas of justice were much more extensive than those of most other philosophers, or perhaps those of statesmen. "The first justice," he says) (De Virtutibus) respects the gods; the "next the demons; then those relating to our country and our parents, and the last the dead, in

" which is included piety, which is either a part of " justice or follows it."

This is the only passage in the works of Aristotle in which mention is made of *gods*, and here he evidently means such gods as were acknowledged by his country. However, the neglect or contempt of these rites of worship, whatever they were, he would have punished. " It is injustice," he adds, (Ib.) " to violate the custom and institution " of our country, and not to obey the laws and the " magistrates." This includes the principle of persecution for religious opinions and practices, which Aristotle, no doubt, held, in common with all the philosophers and magistrates of his time, so that nothing better could reasonably be expected of him.

Thus we have seen the result of the speculation, and laborious researches, of the most acute and sagacious of all the Grecian philosophers, of a man who, with respect both to genius and industry, may be classed among the first of mankind, on these most important subjects. But notwithstanding marks of superior good sense, and discernment, in the writings of Aristotle, we do not find in them any real advance in theological or moral science. And as to any *practical use* of his doctrines, it appears to be something

something less than the world was in possession of before.

As to the great object of heathen philosophy in general, which was to enable men to bear the evils of life, and the fear or the pains of death, he never, that I recollect, so much as mentions the subject; but treats of generation and dissolution merely as natural phenomena, to be explained upon physical principles, but he never regards them in a moral light. On the consequence of death, and a state of retribution after it, he is likewise wholly silent; probably from not believing any thing either of the notions of the vulgar, or the refined speculations of Plato. Had the subjects been much upon his mind, he must have treated of them, and with seriousness, as in themselves highly interesting to himself; as well as to the rest of mankind.

What is peculiarly remarkable in Aristotle, is that though he *reasons* much, and disputes with wonderful subtlety, he seems to have *felt* nothing. He never expresses himself with any warmth, or any degree of sensibility, when he is treating of the most important subjects; but writes concerning God, and the soul, and of virtue and vice, with as much coolness as he describes his plants and animals. How different, in this respect, as well as in many others, are the writings of Aristotle from the Psalms of David, the writings of the prophets, and other devotional and moral articles in the books of scripture, penned by men of no uncommon ability of any kind, but deeply impressed with the importance of the subjects on which they write, and having more knowledge of them. They know infinitely more of God, and of his constant attention to the affairs of men, individuals as well as nations, and therefore they write as if they were really sensible of his presence with them, and his unremitted attention to them, as the proper author of all the good and evil that fell to their lot. They regarded him not only as their moral governor, and final judge, but as their father, and their friend; and thence were led to address themselves to him on all interesting occasions.

What is there, in this respect, in all the heathen writings to compare with the language of the Psalms? To quote a few verses out of thousands, I shall just transcribe the beginning of the 116th. Psalm. *I love the Lord because he has heard my voice, and my supplications. Because he has inclined his ear unto me, therefore will I call upon him as long as I live. The sorrows of death compassed me, and the pains of hell got hold upon me. I found trouble and*

and sorrow, then called I upon the name of the Lord, O Lord I beseech thee, deliver my soul. &c. &c.

I am tempted to add the beginning of the 139th Psalm. *O Lord thou hast searched me and known me. Thou knowest my down sitting and my uprising. Thou understandest my thoughts afar off. Thou compassest my path, and my lying down, and art acquainted with all my ways. For there is not a word in my tongue, but lo, O Lord, thou knowest it altogether. Thou hast beset me behind and before, and laid thine hand upon me. Such knowledge is too wonderful for me. It is high, I cannot attain unto it.*

This is language that comes from the *heart*, implying a feeling sense of the intimate presence, and constant inspection, of God, naturally producing a *direct address* to him, which does not appear ever to have been made by any of the philosophers. Their feelings, therefore, must have been very different. Supposing them to have been the same in *kind*, they must have been unspeakably different in *degree*. Their acknowledgment of the universal presence of God must have been mere speculation, and rested, as we say, in head, but never reached the heart. But this strikes us in every psalm of David.

OF

OF THE

STOICAL PHILOSOPHY OF MARCUS ANTONINUS AND EPICTETUS.

THE Stoic philosophy the founder of which was Zeno, who flourished about three hundred years before Christ, and a little after Aristotle, arose a considerable time after Socrates, and it is on several accounts the most respectable of all the heathen systems, especially as it regards the being and providence of God, and the submission we owe to it, patience in adversity, and resignation to death. It was soon opposed by the doctrine of Epicurus, which made *pleasure*, though not sensual pleasure, but rather the enjoyment of life in general, the great object and end of human life, whereas, according to the Stoics, pleasure of every kind, as well as pain, is to be ranked among things *indifferent*, and not to be attended to in the great rule of life.

When the Grecian philosophy was introduced into Rome, some of the most virtuous and respectable characters embraced that of the Stoics, in preference

ference to any other; especially Cato, and in a later period the emperor Marcus Antoninus, who made what he deemed to be virtue, and whatever he thought to be subservient to the good of his country, more an object than any other of the emperors, or almost any other heathen that we read of. It will, therefore, be well worth while to examine the fundamental principles of this philosophy; as this alone can come in any competition with the christian. And as the fairest specimen of it may be seen in the writings of Marcus Antoninus, and Epictetus, I shall, in this place, confine myself to the examination of their works, in which we may be sure to find the genuine principles of it without any danger of mistake. Seneca indeed, and Arrian came before Marcus Antoninus, and their principles were those of the Stoics. But there is too much of rhetoric in their compositions, especially those of Seneca, whereas the writings of the emperor came, no doubt, from the heart, and express neither more nor less than he really thought. However, I shall subjoin to this section an account of the sentiments of Seneca and Arrian.

SECTION I.

Of God and Providence.

It was a fixed maxim with the Stoics, as it was with Socrates, from whom none of the founders of sects that came after him pretended to differ, that there is a principle of intelligence, wisdom and also of benevolence, directing all the affairs of the world and of men, though they do not ascribe proper *creation* to it. Sometimes they even speak of it in the singular number, though more generally in the plural; believing that, though the principle of intelligence was *one*, it was distributed to several individuals, and indeed to men, and all other intelligent agents.

But none of the philosophers adopted the popular ideas of the gods of their country. Though they sometimes make use of the same *names*, (and this is not frequent) they had a very different idea of their *characters*. In their writings we find nothing of the lewdness, the cruelty, and caprice of the gods of Homer and Virgil; nor do they ever make any apology for rejecting the notions of the common people. This

This unity of principle in all the orders of intelligent beings would, in the opinion of the philosophers, secure the *unity of design* in the whole system that was subordinate to them, and governed by them. "There is," says Marcus Antoninus (Lib. vii. sect. 9.) "one world, one god in all "things, one matter, and one law. Consequently, "reason in all intelligent beings is the same in "all, and truth also is one."

He makes use, though only once, of the name of Jupiter as that of the Supreme Being, when he speaks of the principle of intelligence in all men as derived from one source. "We should live," he says, (Lib. v. sect. 7.) "with the gods; and this "any person will do who preserves his mind in a "disposition to acquiesce in what is appointed "him, and who acts according to that genius, "which Jupiter, having detached it from himself, "gives to every person to be his future guide and "commander, which is every person's mind, or "reason." He evidently considered the sun as a portion of the universal deity, when he says, (Lib. viii. sect. 19.) "the sun, and the other gods, exist "for some purpose or other."

That this universal mind has a perfect knowledge of all things, even of what passes in the minds

of

men, was the belief of the Stoics, as well as of Socrates. "God," says Marcus Antoninus, (Lib. xii. sect. 2.) "sees all minds divested of their co-
"verings and flesh. By his own mind alone he
"sees them as derived from him. If you will do
"the same, you will be freed from much trouble."
For believing that all minds are only parts of one whole, he ascribes to them all much of the same power, as we shall see more particularly hereafter.

He, however, takes it for granted that all good and evil is the dispensation of the gods, and therefore he holds it as a fixed maxim to be thankful for the former, and patiently to bear the latter. "I
"thank God," he says, (Lib. i. sect. 17.) "for
"good grandfathers, good parents, good precep-
"tors, good acquaintance, domestics, and friends,
"and for good of every other kind. If," says he (Lib. vi. sect. 44.) "the gods take no care of the
"world, which it is impiety to believe, why do we
"sacrifice, pray, take oaths, and do other things
"which suppose the gods to be present with us,
"and attentive to us?"

The heathens in general, without excepting any of the philosophers, except Epicurus, were disposed

posed to believe that the gods interposed in the affairs of man, giving him admonitions, and suggestions by dreams, omens, oracles, and various other ways. "With respeet to the gods," say Marcus Antoninus (Lib. i. sect. 17.) "their suggestions, "and the aids, and inspirations that come from "them, nothing hinders my living according to the "rule of nature, unless it be my fault, in not observing those hints from the gods, which are "sometimes obscure."

He seems sometimes, however, to consider such an order of things established from all eternity as would render all prayer, sacrifices, &c. useless. "Whatever happens to you," he says, (Lib. x. sect. 5.) "was destined for you from all eternity. "This" he says, "was done, (Lib. iv. sect. 26.) "by a certain fate." And again, "the series of "causes combined with one another, connects "your existence with that event from all eternity." This, however, is the belief of Jews and Christians, and according to their ideas is not incompatible with prayer. But it is doubtful whether Marcus Antoninus entered into the proper principle of this, so as to make prayer perfectly compatible with his idea of fate. It does not appear that the Stoics in general, any more than other heathen philosophers,

 had

had their minds exercised in prayer, habitual and occasional, in the manner of pious Jews and Christians. We should otherwise have had more of their devotional compositions, similar to those of the psalms of David, and other forms of prayer that occur in the books of scripture. The difference between the heathens and the believers in revelation in this respect is so striking as I observed before, as proves a very different state of mind with respect to a God and providence, whatever may be inferred to the contrary from occasional expressions in their writings.

That every thing that was appointed and directed by the Supreme Being is right, Marcus Antoninus never doubted. "If there be a God," he says, (Lib. ix. sect. 29.) "every thing is right." According to him, this made the existence of any thing properly *evil* absolutely impossible. "Nothing," he says, (Lib x. sect. 6.) "can be hurtful that is good for the whole; and every thing in the universe must be good for *it*. This is common to the nature of every thing, and the world must have it in the greatest degree, because there is nothing external to itself to force any thing noxious upon it." This consideration is with us also an argument for the unchangeable

ble goodness, and other attributes, of God, the evidence of which we see in the works of nature. We say that, since there are evident marks of *benevolence* in what we experience and see around us, a principle of *malevolence*, which is opposite to it, cannot be admitted. Every thing, therefore, must have been designed for the best, whether at present we can see it to be so or not. And as there is nothing in nature superior to this benevolent supreme intelligence, this system, tending in all respects to good, must be perpetual.

That this system is in a progressive state of continual improvement was not the doctrine of the Stoics. It was rather their opinion that, after a certain period, every thing would return to the state in which it had been before; so that nothing would be gained by their perpetual revolutions. In this their system coincided with that of the Hindoos, and the oriental philosophers. This seems to be intimated by Marcus Antoninus. "We should bear in mind," he says, (Lib. ii. sect. 14.) "two things, one that all things have "been from eternity in a perpetual round. There "is in it no difference between seeing the same "things a hundred years, two hundred years, or in "a longer duration." How dull and unpleasant is

 this

this prospect compared to that which is suggested in our scriptures; according to which nothing will ever return to the state in which it has been before, but every thing will continually advance in improvement, without, however, ever reaching *perfection*, which must ever be the exclusive prerogative of the Supreme Being.

The duty of absolute submission to the divine will, and the order of nature, as coincident with it, cannot be inculcated more forcibly than it is by the Stoics. "Man," says Marcus Antoninus, (Lib. xii. sect. 12.) "should do nothing but what God "himself would approve, and he should receive "willingly whatever he assigns him. With re-"spect to every thing that is agreeable to nature, "the gods are not to be blamed, for they do nothing "wrong with design." "The principal article of "piety towards the gods," says Epictetus, (sect. 31.) "is to have just opinions concerning them, "as that they exist, and administer every thing "well and rightly, and that it is our business to "obey them, and acquiesce voluntarily in every "thing that takes place, as being disposed for the "best." Treating of death, Marcus Antoninus says, (Lib. vi. sect. 10.) "If every thing be order-"ed by providence, I venerate the supreme ruler, "and

"and, depending upon him, am unmoved." From his opinion of the duty of submission to the divine will, he excellently observes, (Lib. ix. sect. 40.) "the gods either have power, or no power. If "they have no power, why do you pray? If they "have power, why do you not rather pray that you "may be without anxiety about an event, than that "the event may not take place?" This may instruct even a christian.

It was the opinion of all the heathens, from the earliest to the latest times, that it was right, and even necessary, to adhere to the religious rites of their ancestors; since the prosperity of the state they thought depended upon it. On this principle, absurd and groundless as it apparently is, it was that the wisest and best of the heathens acted. It was on this principle that Marcus Antoninus, Trajan, and some others, the best disposed of the Roman emperors, wished to exterminate the christians, in order that the rites of the antient religion might not grow into disuse, to the endangering of the state. "It is every person's duty," says Epictetus, (sect. 31.) "to make libations, offer sa-"crifices, and first fruits, according to the custom "of his country, not sordidly, or negligently, nor "above our means."

The good sense, however, of Marcus Antoninus taught him that there might be an excess, and superstition, in this external worship. For he commends a person (Lib. vi. sect. 30.) for being "religious without superstition." He also says (Lib. vi. sect. 23.) "In all things pray for the divine "aid, and consider that there is no difference how "long we are doing this. Three hours thus passed may suffice." He does not, however, say for what space of time these three hours would suffice.

Like Socrates, the emperor connected the practice of morality with religion; though with this, the religious rites of states, those on which their prosperity was thought to depend, had no connection whatever. "It is of much consequence," he says, (Lib. x. sect. 8.) "to remember that there are "gods, and that they do not wish men to deceive "them, or to flatter them, but to imitate them. "He that fears pain, (Lib. ix sect. 1.) fears what "must be in the world, and this is impious; and "he who follows pleasure will not refrain from injustice, which is certainly impious."

SECTION

Section II.

Of the Human Soul.

Hitherto we have found the principles of the Stoics what may be called *sublime*, and in a great degree rational, as there is but little to correct in their ideas of the supreme intelligence, of his universal providence, or the obligation they maintain that all men are under to conform to its will, and acquiesce in its decisions, as necessarily right and good. But we shall now find them deviating very far from truth and common sense, and leading themselves and others into errors of a practical nature, as we proceed to consider their ideas concerning the *mind of man*, the disposition to be cultivated in it, and the essentials of moral virtue.

The Stoics held the doctrine of *three principles in man*, viz. his *body*, consisting of gross matter, the principle of mere *animal life*, called by them (πνευμα) or (ψυχη,) and the proper *intellectual principle*, called (νους.) The difference between men and other animals appeared to them to be so great, that they could not believe the latter to be possessed of the highest principle of human nature.

But as men have every thing that belongs to brutes, in which they acknowledge some thing superior to mere *matter*, they were under a necessity of making the component parts of man to be three.

Moreover, as they considered all matter as fundamentally the same, though forming different substances, they conceived the animal principle to be the same in all, flowing from a common source, to animate particular bodies for a time, and then, like the breath to which it was generally compared, mixed with the origin from which it was derived.

In like manner, having no idea of a proper *creation*, i. e. *out of nothing*, they considered the highest principle in man, viz. that of intelligence, as the same in all, derived from the same source; and this they conceived to be the supreme intelligence, which disposed and directs the affairs of the whole universe, and like the principle of animal life, they held that, being detached from this source at the birth of every man, it was absorbed into it again after his death, as a drop of water (to use a comparison that is frequent with them) is absorbed and lost in the ocean. Consequently, its separate existence, and separate consciousness, then vanished.

Accord-

According to this philosophy, therefore, the souls of men are so many portions of the divinity; and this led the professors of it to ascribe to them the properties and powers of divinity, making them sufficient for their own happiness, independently of every thing external to them. And, as the supreme intelligence is incapable of suffering from evil of any kind, they transferred this extraordinary power to the soul; maintaining that nothing foreign to itself could affect it without its own consent, so that it is in every man's power to be completely happy, whatever his outward circumstances may be.

This sentiment, which has an air of great sublimity, tended to inspire the Stoics with a sense of native dignity, rendering them superior to every thing mean and base; but it excluded humility, and many amiable and useful virtues, peculiarly adapted to the state of society with beings equally imperfect with themselves. Their sentiments however, on this subject so nearly connected with morals, led them to express themselves with respect to the common accidents of life in a manner that, with a little qualification, is truly admirable and edifying. But when taken literally their language justly shocks a christian, who feels his own weakness, and is thereby disposed to compassionate the weakness and infirmities of others; the most amiable, and in the present state of things, one of the most useful of all virtues.

On the subject of the different component parts of man Marcus Antoninus expresses himself as follows: "Man, (Lib. xii. sect. 2.) consists of flesh, "the animal principle, (πνευματιον) and the governing principle (ἡγεμονικον.) The (πνευμα) "is breath, or air, (ανεμος) nor is it always the "same, but is drawn in and emitted. You consist, (Lib. xii. sect. 3.) of three parts, the body, "the (πνευματιον,) and the mind, (νους). The "two former are so far yours, as that they are "committed to your care, but the third only is "properly yours." For the intellectual part of man was considered as so much superior to the other two, as to deserve to be alone called *a man's self.* And on several occasions we shall find that the two other parts were thought to be as much foreign to a man as if they did not belong to him at all, any more than other parts of the external world.

The unity of these three elements of which every man consists, is thus described by Marcus Antoninus, "One living principle (ψυχη) (Lib. ix. sect. 8.) "is distributed to all irrational animals, and one in-

"telligent

"telligent living principle (νοερα ψυχη) to all ra-"tional ones, just as to the several elements there "is one and the same earth. We all see and live "with one light, and breathe one air. There is "(Lib. xii. sect. 30.) one light of the sun, though "it be distributed upon different things, one com-"mon nature, though distributed into various dif-"ferent bodies, one (ψυχη,) though distributed to "innumerable peculiar natures, and one intelli-"gent principle (νοερα ψυχη) though it seems to "be divided."

The idea which the Stoics entertained of the native dignity, and superior powers, of the human mind flowed necessarily from their opinion of its origin and final destination; but it corresponds very little with experience, and is wholly discordant with the principles of revelation. "You forget," says Marcus Antoninus, (Lib. xii. sect. 26.) "that "the mind of every man is God, and flowed from "the divinity." And again, (Lib. iv. sect. 14.) "Thou art part of the universe, and will vanish "into that which produced thee, or rather by some "intervening change, thou wilt be received into "the seminal reason (λογον σπερματικον) i. e. the "the source of all reason."

These

These ideas of the great power, and natural independence, of the mind were suitable to the opinion of its high origin and final destination, as having been originally part of the supreme universal intelligence, and destined to be absorbed into it, and to become part of it again. "It belongs," says Marcus Antoninus, (Lib. vii. sect. 55.) "to the mind "to be free from error and defect. Neither fire, "nor external violence, nor calumny, nor any "thing else can reach the mind when, like a sphere, "it is compact within itself (Lib. viii. sect. 41.) "The soul endued with reason has the following "powers, (Lib. xi. sect. 1.) it sees itself, it forms "and limits itself, it makes itself whatever it pleas-"es. Whatever fruit it produces it reaps itself; "whereas other persons gather the fruits of trees, "and also whatever is produced from animals. "It always gains its purpose, at whatever time its "life terminates; so that it is not, as in a dance, "or a play, in which the action is sometimes inter-"rupted by incidents, and is therefore imperfect. "But wherever it is taken, what precedes is com-"plete and perfect; so that I may say, I have eve-"ry thing that belongs to me within me. Add to "this, the mind traverses the whole world, and "what surrounds it. It contemplates its form,

"and

"and looking forward into eternity, it considers "the renovation of the universe at certain inter-"vals."

An essential prerogative of the mind of man, and of the most use in the conduct of life, the Stoics considered to be its *command of thought*, and by this means its total independence on every thing foreign to itself; since it is under no necessity of giving any attention to them. "How can opini-"ons," says Marcus Antoninus (Lib. vii. sect. 2.) "be abolished, unless thoughts suitable to them be "extinguished, which you may for that purpose "call up whenever you please. I can think of "any thing that I have occasion for; and if I can, "why should my mind be disturbed?"

Thus these philosophers flattered themselves with the idea of their happiness being wholly independent on any thing foreign to the mind, and that it became them to maintain a perfect indifference towards every thing that is the object of affection, or respect, to other men. "If you behave" says Epictetus (sect. 15.) "with becoming indifference "towards children, wife, the magistrate, riches, "&c. &c. you will be worthy of being a guest of "the gods; but if you can despise all these things "that are foreign to yourself, you will not only be

"a com-

"a companion with them, but a god yourself.
"Thus Diogenes, Heraclitus, and others like
'them, deserve to be called, and really were, *di-*
"*vine.*" It is surely hardly possible to carry extravagance and absurdity farther than this; so far, however, we see that a false philosophy, pursued to its natural consequences, can carry men from every thing that we are taught by daily experience and observation of common life. And yet these were men of deep thought and reflection, and both Epictetus and Marcus Antoninus lived in the world, and had to do with men and their affairs

SECTION III.

Of Virtue and Vice.

The great use of religion, and of moral philosophy, is to furnish the mind with proper rules of life, by the observance of which we shall best secure our own happiness, and be the most disposed to promote that of others, to enable us to bear the evils of life with the least pain, and the prospect of death without terror. On all these three heads, therefore, I shall examine the merit of the Stoical philosophy, and compare it with the christian.

The

dignified sentiments maintained by the Stoics concerning the human soul lead us to expect great elevation of mind with respect to virtue; and in this we shall no tbe disappointed, as far as virtue in their ideas of it extended; and it comprehended every thing that relates to the due government of the passions, all the relative duties, and those that affect the intercourse between man and man. They also made happiness to depend entirely on the practice of virtue, independent on any foreign consideration, such as the fear of punishment, the hope of reward, or the opinion of others, expressed in praise or censure.

Marcus Antoninus, having observed that it is in the power of man to be happy in any situation, and especially in one that suits him, says (Lib. v. sect. 36.) "If you ask what this proper situation is, I answer, that it consists in good morals, a good disposition, and good actions. It is a pleasure to a "man (Lib. viii. sect. 26.) to do what suits his nature, and it suits the nature of man to be kind to "his countrymen, to command the emotions of "his senses, to distinguish what is probable in "what is before him, to contemplate the nature of "the universe, and the things that are agreeable to "it. Do nothing" he says, (Lib. xi. sect. 18.) "for

"for the sake of admiration, but be the same when "alone as if your were before others." For he justly observes (Lib. xii. sect. 4.) "We fear more "what others think of us, than what we think of "ourselves." Agreeable to this, Epictetus says (sect. 23.) "If your thoughts be employed in ex-"ternal things, and you wish to please any person, "you err from the path of life; whereas in all ca-"ses remember that you are a philosopher, and "that you appear so to yourself, though not to "others."

The Stoics carried the principle of disinterestedness to the highest pitch, beyond the bounds of reason or nature, expecting no reward for their virtues either in this life, or any other, except the satisfaction of their own minds; and this was short of any proper pleasurable sensation. For, according to their general system, nothing of this kind ought to be indulged. "When you confer a favour" says Marcus Antoninus (Lib. ix. sect. 42.) "is not this "sufficient, without any reward? Does the eye "require a reward for seeing, or the feet for walk-"ing? So man, who is made to do good, should "be satisfied with the good that he does."

These extremely rigid maxims, so much above the comprehension of the vulgar, led them to consider

sider the practice of virtue as the peculiar privilege of philosophers, and real happiness as much more so. For who besides philosophers could be expected to despise every thing that was foreign to themselves, and to consider every thing on which the comfort of life depends as included in this class; and without this there is, according to them, neither real virtue or true happiness, as will be more evident in the farther developement of their principles.

Some philosophers were poor, as Epictetus himself, who was even some time in servitude; and in an age in which books were scarce and dear, and learning not easily attained, some of them might not be able to read. In this case Marcus Antoninus says, (Lib. viii. cap. 8.) "If you cannot read, "you can abstain from abuse, even of the ungrate- "ful, and also be kind to them. You need not be "heard to complain of your situation, or envy "that of others." Happily, however, these virtues and every other may be attained without philosophy.

Unhappily, the Stoics considered every thing that is foreign to the calm dictates of reason, all emotions and passions, as belonging to mere animal nature; seeing that men have them in common with brutes. They, therefore, thought it a point of magnanimity and duty in man to suppress every thing of this kind with respect to others, as well as themselves. Do not," says Marcus Antoninus, (Lib. vii. sect. 43.) "join others in their lamentati-"ons, or be moved by them." Epictetus, however, makes some little allowance for the weakness of human nature when he says (sect. 16.) "If you "see a friend in distress, accommodate yourself to "him so far as to lament and groan along with him, "but take care that you groan not inwardly."

These maxims, I need not say, are as remote from the dictates of nature, as they are from the precepts of scripture, which bids us to be *kindly affectioned one to another, with brotherly love*, and from this principle *to rejoice with them that rejoice, and to weep with them that weep*. How can men be supposed to *act*, but as prompted by their *feelings?*

Though Marcus Antoninus advises to do good to a man's fellow citizens, and even to the ungrateful, it was not, according to his principles, to be dictated by any *affection*, as that of *love*, but only because it was the part of man, and became him to act in this manner; as it was for the eye to see, or the feet to walk. But christianity knows nothing of the

the distinction of the different component parts of man, and the natural superiority of one of them to the rest. Paul, though he expresses a wish that his brethren might be *sanctified in body, soul and spirit*, it was only in allusion to the three fold division of man above mentioned, which was familiar to the Greeks, to whom he was writing, desiring that, whatever they considered as belonging to man, or part of him, it might be sanctified, as a suitable temple for the spirit of God. He was not declaring his own principles, as a Jew, or a Christian.

The opinion which the Stoics maintained of the superior excellence of the intellectual principle in all men was such, that they considered every emotion or passion that led to vice as foreign to it, as arising only from the principle that is common to men and brutes; and therefore not from any thing that was properly a man's self. In consequence of this, they professed to have no indignation against the vices of men, but considered them like evils, and inconveniences of any other kind, at which it does not become any man to be disturbed, being agreeable to the order of the nature.

Accordingly, Marcus Antoninus having observed that we have no reason to complain of the gods with respect to any thing that befalls us, adds (Lib. xii. sect. 12.) " Neither are men to be complained of. " For neither do they offend willingly. It is the part " of man (Lib. vii. sect. 22.) to love those who of- " fend them; and this he will do if he recollect " that all men are related, and that when they of- " fend, it is when they do not know it, or do it a- " gainst their wills. When I consider that the " person who injures me (Lib. ii. sect. 1.) is a par- " taker of the same intellect, and portion of the " divinity, that I cannot be injured by him, that he " has no power to draw me into any thing disho- " nest, I cannot be angry with him, or hate him."

The Stoics were led into these sentiments, and this conduct, by considering every man as wholly independent on every other, each being separately sufficient for his own happiness, and incapable of interfering with that of any other. " Does any " person offend me," says Marcus Antoninus (Lib. v. sect. 25.) " let him look to it. He has his own " dispositions and actions, and I have what nature " wills me to have, and I do what is agreeable to " nature." Again he says, (Lib. iv. cap. 26.) " Does any person injure me. No, he injures " himself. If you suffer (Lib. ix. sect. 42.) " through fraudulent, faithless, injurious, persons,

" consi-

"consider that there must be such men in the "world, and you will bear with them. When "you take any thing ill (Lib. xii. sect. 25.) you "forget that every thing takes place according to "the nature of the universe. If we consider these "things only as evils which depend upon our own "wills, we shall see no reason for blameing, or bear-"ing ill will to, any man."

Besides this great indifference to the vices of other persons, as injuring only themselves, that of fornication was never considered by any heathens philosophers, or others, as one, any farther than it was found to be injurious. This is evident from the advice that Epictetus gives (sect. 33.) "Ab-"stain as much as you can from venery before "marriage. If not, do it as the laws permit, but "do not find fault with others who are not conti-"nent, or boast that you are so."

How short is this of the purity required of christians, who are taught to consider fornicators, as well as adulterers, thieves, &c. excluded from the kingdom of heaven, and how little attention must these philosophers have given to the natural consequences of venereal indulgence without the bounds of marriage; how ill it qualifies men to be affectionate husbands, and fathers, and that in many cases it must indispose men to marriage in general. There was also this inconsistence in their maxims in this respect, that fornication was always reckoned infamous in the female sex; so that women of character never associated with known prostitutes. The christian catalogue of both virtues and vices is far more copious than that of the heathens, which was defective with respect to duties of every kind, those that are commonly said men owe to themselves, and to society, as well as those that we owe to God, notwithstanding that of submission to his will, which is one of the great excellencies of the maxims of the Stoics; as this was founded chiefly on its being merely taken for granted, without considering any particular evidence of it, that every thing in the universe, and the government of it, must be right. For the wisdom of providence in the permission or appointment of evil is never mentioned by Marcus Antoninus. That such things as evils of every kind *must be*, is the amount of all that he says on the subject; and that they do not affect any person who considers these as foreign to himself. He says nothing of the beneficial tendency of the things that we call evil, and complain of in the system, obvious as this tendency is now seen to be. Marcus

cus

cus Antoninus would *bear* tribulation, but the apostle Paul *rejoices* in it.

The maxims of the heathens were still more defective with respect to sufficient *motives* to the practice of virtue, in the fear of future punishment, and the prospect of future reward; and all other motives will have but little hold on the bulk of mankind, especially if they be already engaged in bad habits. On such persons, a disinterested respect to virtue, so much insisted upon by Marcus Antoninus, cannot be expected to have any influence.

SECTION IV.

Of the various Evils of Life.

Another great use of religion and philosophy is to enable men to bear the various evils incident to them in life with as little inconvenience as possible; and accordingly this was a principal object of the philosophy of the Stoics, far more than it was with any of the other sects. In this respect their pretensions went very high indeed, far, as we shall see, beyond the bounds of reason and nature; so that daily experience, one would have thought, must have convinced them of their mistake. Notwithstanding this, they resolutely maintained their favourite, and indeed fundamental maxims, of indifference to every thing foreign to themselves, (meaning the intellectual principle in them only) which enjoined patience under, and even insensibility to, all that mankind in general complain of, and call *evils*.

On this principle they held that, without its own consent, the mind could not be affected by any thing. "I learned," says Marcus Antoninus (Lib. 1. sect. 8.) "of Apollonius to regard nothing besides mere reason, to be the same in the most "acute pain, in the loss of children, and in diseas-"es of long continuance." So also Epictetus says, (sect. 1.) "If the things that disturb you be "not in your power, have it ready to say, This is "nothing to me. And if you consider that only "as yours which is yours, and what is foreign to "you as foreign to you, no person will constrain "or hinder you. You will complain of no man. "You will do nothing against your will. You "will have no enemy, nor suffer any thing disa-"greeable to you."

This

This opinion of the nature and powers of the mind, and of things that were, or were not, foreign to themselves, an opinion on which so much depended, they conceived to be easily formed by those who had been taught to philosophize, so as to be readily applied on all occasions. It was only the office of *thought*, than which nothing is more easy to *mind*, the property of which is to think. In this respect they made no difference between the most painful sensations and impressions, corporeal or mental, though in these we find that the mind is absolutely passive; they supposing all sensations and emotions were to be referred to the merely animal part of man, on which they main tained that the mind was wholly independent; so that whatever impression might be made from without, it was in its power to relieve itself.

Consequently, they held that pleasure and pain of every kind are not to be classed among things that are either good or evil. Marcus Antoninus says (Lib. ii. cap. 11.) "Life and death, honour "and ignominy, pain and pleasure, wealth and po-"verty, may be equally considered as good or evil; "since they are neither honourable nor disho-"nourable, and are therefore neither good nor "evil*." But the difficulty consists in being fully convinced of this, and regarding that as indifferent in contradiction to the actual feelings of themselves, as well as of the rest of mankind. Of this, however, they made very light.

"Reject opinion," says Marcus Antoninus, (Lib. xii. sect. 25.) "and you are safe; and what "hinders your doing this, when any thing happens "that is disagreeable to you? you forget that this "happens

* *There is a passage in the Table of Cebes, who was a disciple of Socrates, in which this sentiment of life and death, health and sickness, being to be classed among things indifferent to happiness occurs. But it must have been added by some person who, if not a Stoic, must have lived long after the time of this Cebes. "Life," he says, is not to be classed "among the* goods *or the* evils; *because it is enjoy-"ed alike by those who live well, and those who live "ill. The same may be said of cutting and burn-"ing; for these operations are usefully employed by "those who are sick and those who are well. Nei-"ther is death an absolute evil; because it is some-"times preferred to life by the brave; nor health, "or sickness, riches, or any other seeming advan-"tage; because they are often of no real use."*

" happens according to the nature of the universe. " Take away opinion," he says (Lib. iv. sect. 7.) ' and complaint is removed. Whatever does not " make a man worse, or his conduct worse, cannot " injure him internally or externally," And again, (Lib. vii. cap. 14.) " If I do not consider a- " ny thing that befalls me as an evil, I am not in- " jured, and it depends upon myself whether I think " so or not. How easy," says he, (Lib. v. sect. 2.) " to remove every imagination that is troublesome " or inconvenient, so as to preserve the mind in " perfect tranquility. In pain (Lib. viii. cap. 28.) " the soul may preserve its tranquility, and not " think it to be an evil. Every thing of the nature " of opinion, inclination, and appetite, is within us, " where nothing that is evil can come. Remove " imagination," he says, addressing himself ", and " it is in my power that no vice, no irregular de- " sire, no perturbation, exist in my mind; but, re- " garding every thing as it really is, to make use of " it according to its value. Remember that this ' power is given to you by nature. So Epictetus says (sect. 30.) " No person can hurt you unless " you will. Then only are you injured, when you " think you are so."

In a more particular manner they made light of every

every thing that affected the *body* only, for which, as consisting of brute matter, they professed the greatest contempt, as if it had borne no relation whatever to the mind, which they considered as the only proper seat of good or evil, true pleasure or pain. "Nothing," says Marcus Antoninus, (Lib. iv. sect. 39.) "that is an evil to you, depends upon "any change that takes place in that in which you "are inclosed. If the body be cut, burned, or "putrefy, only let that part of a man which forms "its opinion concerning it be at rest, that is, "not consider that as good or evil, which may hap-"pen either to good or bad men. For whatever "happens alike to him that lives agreeably to na-"ture, or contrary to it, is a matter of indifference. "You may pass your life (Lib. vii. sect. 68.) with-"out injury, and with the greatest cheerfulness, "though wild beasts tear the limbs of the body "that surrounds you, and adheres to you."

The language in which they sometimes express this indifference to the body is amusing, and might have been said by way of ridicule of their system. "Pain," says Marcus Antoninus, (Lib. viii. sect. 28.) "is an evil to the body. If it is so, let the bo-"dy look to it. As to the limbs of the body, (Lib. "vii. sect. 33.) if they be in pain, let them take

"care

"care of it, if they can do any thing." Again (Lib. xii. sect. 1.) "Let the flesh with which you "are surrounded mind its own sufferings." "If "the reason," says Epictetus (sect. 18.) "forebode "any ill, immediately reply, it may be to your bo-"dy, your reputation, your children, or your wife. "Every thing fortunate is intended for me, if I "please. For whatever happens to me, is in my "power, and I may derive advantage from it."

However, besides this great sheet anchor, as it may be called, of the Stoics, by which they procured their tranquility in all the storms of life, viz. their idea of the absolute independence of the mind upon every thing external to it, and its sufficiency for its own happiness, they occasionally mention other considerations not peculiar to themselves, some of more, and some of less, weight. Among others, Marcus Antoninus says, (Lib. vii. sect. 33.) "If pain con-"not be borne, it will cease, and if it be of long "continuance, it may be borne; and in the mean "time the mind, by means of its opinion, may "preserve its tranquility."

Another of his resources is not so reasonable. "Think with yourself," he says (Lib. viii. sect. 36.) "that nothing past or future, but only that "which

"which is present can be the cause of uneasiness "to you." This is by no means true with respect to beings capable of reflection, whose happiness or misery necessarily depends much more on the past and the future than on the present moment. It is only a brute, or a child, to which this observation is applicable, nor even to them completely, or long.

One rule of Epictetus, however, is truly valuable, if it could be applied. But the Stoics always imagined that much more was in their power than really was so. "Do not (sect. 8.) seek to find things "as you wish them to be, but wish for that which "actually is, and you will pass your life in tranqui-"lity." The great difficulty in this case (but to this the Stoics gave no attention) is in the application of such a rule; and other principles, out of the sphere of their philosophy, but comprehended in those of christianity, are necessary to assist us in this.

This great excellence of character, which raises some men so much above the level of their species, and which rendered them superior to all the evils of life, and also to the fear of death, the Stoics ascribed wholly to philosophy; so that it required much study and reflection to attain it, though afterwards the exercise of it was easy. "The time "of

" of human life," says Marcus Antoninus (Lib. ii. sect. 17.) " is a point; nature is in a continual " flux, the senses are obscure, the body liable to " corruption, &c. &c. the only thing" (that is of value) " is philosophy, which consists in preserv" ing the mind intire, superior to pleasure or pain, " self-sufficient, having nothing to do with what " others do or do not do, and receiving the things " that befall them as coming from the same source " with themselves." " It is a mark," says Epictetus (sect. 48.) " of the common people to look " for loss or gain from what is external to them, " but the philosopher expects nothing but from " himself. The proof that he is a philosopher, is, " that he censures no person, commands no per" son, complains of no man, never boasts of him" self, as a person of any consequence. If he meets " with obstacles from his acquaintance he blames " only himself. If any person praise him he laughs " at him, and if he be censured he does not excuse " himself." &c.

If only such persons as these be philosophers, they will never be very numerous. Indeed, we must not look for them among *men*, not even those who make the greatest profession and boast of this very philosophy; because it could not be in their

power

power to divest themselves of the common principles of human nature. We see, however, in these extremely absurd maxims, how far metaphysical or general principles can carry men, at least in speculation; and therefore of what importance it is to form just ones, agreeable to the real principles of human nature; for such only can lead to the proper duty and happiness of man.

That the Stoics, however, found more difficulty than they were willing in general to allow, in reducing their maxims to practice, appears from their frequently inculcating the necessity of having proper rules, or remedies, at hand for every case that might occur. "As surgeons," says Marcus Antoninus (Lib. iii. sect. 13.) "have their instruments "ready for every operation, so have you your max- "ims ready, by the help of which you may distin- "guish divine and human things," meaning probably things within our power, and those that were out of it. "There is no retirement (Lib. iv. sect. "3.) so complete as that into one's own mind, espe- "cially if it be well stored with maxims, by the con- "sideration of which it may attain perfect tranquili- "ty. And by this means it is in a man's power to "remove every cause of uneasiness." "Whate- "ver occurs to you," says Epictetus (sect. 10.) "have

" have some principle ready to oppose to it. If " you see a beautiful boy or girl, have recourse to " continence, if labour the enduring of it, if re- " proach patience. By this means appearances " will not mislead you." " In pain let this consi- " deration be at hand," says Marcus Antoninus, (Lib. vii. sect. 64.) " that it is not disgraceful, or " makes the governing power" (the mind) " at all the " worse, and that nothing that is either material, or " that relates to other persons, can injure it."

How greatly superior, and how much better adapted to the real principles of human nature, and the common feelings of men, are the consolations of our religion, to those of this philosophy! In the scriptures the idea of the Divine Being is that of the universal parent, our father in heaven, who never afflicts his children but for their benefit. *He does not*, we read, *afflict willingly, nor grieves the children of men. Yea as a father pitieth his children, the Lord pitieth them that fear him. He knoweth their frame and remembers that they are dust.* With respect to the wicked, he is represented as forbearing to punish with severity, waiting for their repentance and reformation, which is the sole object of the discipline to which they are exposed; *not being willing that any should perish, but that all should come to repentance.*

P. These

These sentiments are such as all men may feel the force of, and are therefore adapted to common use. Christianity also holds out a sufficient reward for all our sufferings, when they are borne with a proper temper; and of this the Stoics taught nothing. *Afflictions*, as the apostle says, *are not joyous but grievous, nevertheless they work out for us a far more exceeding, even an eternal weight of glory; while they make us to look not at the things that are seen, which are temporary, but at the things that are unseen, which are eternal.*

It is not among the Stoics, or any heathens, that we must look for such truly consoling sentiments as these. With these helps, christians are enabled to endure affliction not only with patience, which was all that the Stoics pretended to, but with joy: and accordingly the apostles exhort their fellow christians *to rejoice in tribulation; in every thing to give thanks. Count it all joy says the apostle James,* (Chap. i. v. 2.) *when ye fall into divers trials; knowing that the trial of your faith worketh patience. But let patience have her perfect work, that you may be perfect and intire, wanting nothing*— (v. 12.) *Blessed is the man that endureth temptation: for when he is tried he shall receive the crown of life, which the Lord has promised to them that love him.*

SECTION

Section V.

Of Death.

Of all the evils of life *death* is the natural termination; but it is likewise the same with respect to all the enjoyments of it, and what is more, of all our future *hopes*, if we have nothing to look to beyond it. On this account it has always been classed in the catalogue of the *evils* to which men are subject, and one from which no man, whatever may have been his rank or situation in life, can be exempt.

The apprehension of this universal catastrophe would oppress the mind much more than it generally does, if the *time*, and other *circumstances*, attending it were known to us. But these being unknown, and uncertain, and all men having their thoughts engaged in the pursuit of their several objects, and also naturally disposed to flatter themselves, they seldom think of death till the very near approach of it; and then they are often wholly insensible of it; so that their suffering from it at the time is generally inconsiderable.

Still, however, the consideration of death must often throw a cloud over the brightest prospects of many men who reflect on their situation, and especially those whose lot in life is the most pleasing to them; and, in general, tend to abate the sanguine views and expectations with which persons generally enter upon life. On these accounts a remedy for the fear of death has always been considered as a most desireable thing, and an important article in religion and philosophy. It was so more particularly with the Stoics, as is evident from their frequent mention of it, and the various arguments they urge to reconcile the minds of men to it. Some of them are valuable, and as far as they go, satisfactory; especially that to which they have constant recourse, as flowing directly from the fundamental principle of their system, viz. the submission that we owe to the established order of nature and providence, which we cannot alter, and which we must take for granted is right.

"To die," says Marcus Antoninus (Lib. ii. sect. 11.) "is not grievous, since there are gods, "who will not involve thee in any thing that is evil. "If there were no gods, or if they gave no attenti-"on to the affairs of men, it would not be worth "while to live in such a world. But there are gods,

"gods, and they do take care of human affairs, and "they have put it into every man's power not to "fall into any evil. We should meet death," he says (Lib. ii. sect. 17.) "with a benevolent and "placid mind, as a dissolution of those elements of "which every animal consists. And if nothing "extraordinary happens to these elements, which "are continually changing into one another, it is "no subject of dread, because it is according to "nature, and nothing is an evil that is agreeable "to nature."

One use of the expectation of death is well pointed out by Epictetus, "Let death," says he (sect. 21.) "exile, and every thing that is trouble-"some, be always present to your thoughts, and "especially death, and you will have no mean "thoughts, nor desire any thing inordinately."

Some of the Stoical arguments against the fear of death are not equally satisfactory with that above mentioned, especially that which Marcus Antoninus alleges with respect to evils in general, though he applies it more particularly to the consideration of death, viz. that nothing really interests us besides what is actually present. "In death," he says (Lib. ii. sect. 14.) "we only lose the present,

" which is the same to all persons; for what is past " or future cannot be the subject of life. This " makes the longest life equal to the shortest." On this idea he enlarges in a manner that is truly extraordinary, in a man of general good sense, and disposed to reflection. " Though you should " live," he says, " three thousand years, or more " than ten times as long, you should remember " that no person can have more of this life, or of " any other life, than he really has. It is the same " thing, therefore, whether you have the longest or " the shortest life, since the present is the same to all; " so that what is lost is only momentary."

" If any of the gods," he says (Lib. iv. sect. 47.) " should tell you that you must die either this day " or the next, you would think it a matter of indif- " ference which to chuse, unless you were the most " abject of men. In like manner, neither would " you think it of consequence whether you lived " a thousand years, or died to-morrow. He who " thinks (Lib. xii. sect. 35.) that whatever is season- " able is good, will think there is no difference whe- " ther he perform more or fewer actions agreeable " to reason, and whether he contemplate the uni- " verse a longer or a shorter space of time. To " him death cannot be formidable."

In

In this sentiment, however, the emperor would not have the concurrence of mankind in general. They consider life as valuable, and would, therefore, prefer a longer to a shorter one; and no doubt he himself notwithstanding this reasoning, would have done so too, provided (as we may presume in his case) his prospects, in the continuance of life and of power, had been promising.

What makes the apprehension of death distressing to some persons of a melancholy turn of mind, is their connecting with it things that do not properly belong to it; being things that at the time they cannot have any knowledge or feeling of, as the circumstances attending a funeral, being inclosed in a coffin, being put under ground, and there putrifying, and perhaps devoured by worms, &c. &c. On this subject the emperor very properly says (Lib. ii. sect. 12.) "If we separate from "death every thing that does not necessarily belong "to it, and which usually make it an object of ter-"ror, there is nothing in it but the work of na-"ture; and whoever dreads any thing in nature "is a child. But death is not only the work of na-"ture, but a thing that is of use in the system of "nature, and it is in a man's power to consider "the relation that the principal part of him bears to "God, and what is to be the condition of that "part when it shall be released from the body."

In this he alludes to the philosophical principle of the absorption of all inferior intelligences into the great universal intelligence. But neither he, or any other heathen philosopher, had, or could have, an unshaken belief in that doctrine, little consolation as it can afford. For what is a drop of water (which is their usual comparison) when absorbed in the ocean!

Besides, the Stoics as well as all the other philosophers often express doubts on the subject; like Socrates, putting the supposition, that death is either an entire dispersion of all the elements of which man consists, which puts a period to all consciousness, or that absorption of the soul into the soul of the universe which puts an end to all separate individual consciousness, and which cannot be very different from it. "If," says Marcus Antoninus (Lib. vi. sect. 10.) "every thing is to be "dissipated, why should I think of any thing but "being, some way or other, reduced to earth; and "why should I be disturbed at this? Do what I "will, this dispersion will come some time or

"other

"other. If after death (Lib. iii. sect. 3.) you be "deprived of all sense, you will likewise lose all "sense of pleasure and pain. You will then cease "to be a slave to the worst part of yourself. But "is not that which was enslaved the better part of "you, when the one is intellectual and a genius, "and the other mud and corruption? Wait your "death (Lib. v. sect. 33.) with tranquility, whe-"ther it be an extinction of being, or a removal. "Till that time come, be content to worship the "gods, to do good to men, to bear with them, and "keep at a distance from them, remembering that "every thing foreign to yourself is neither yours, "nor in your power."

This supposition of the two possible consequences of death, so frequent with the heathen philosophers, and with the Stoics as much as any other, certainly shews an unsteadiness of opinion on the subject, and that little consolation was in fact derived from it. No such uncertainty is expressed by Jesus, the apostles, or any christian. With them the belief of a resurrection was as unshaken as that of death, and it operated accordingly, relieving them from all anxiety on the subject, and enabling them ever to rejoice in the prospect of exchanging this life for a better.

On the subject of *self murder*, the Stoics seem to have had no settled opinion; some times maintaining, as the emperor seems to do, that it is the duty of every man to remain in the station in which providence has placed him, till he receives an order from the same power to quit it, by which must be meant, something foreign to a man's own will, or inclination, as by disease, or violence. But if we judge by the practice of some of the most distinguished of the sect, as that of Zeno himself, Plato, and others, they considered it as an act of great heroism, especially becoming a man who must otherwise live in ignominy; notwithstanding their maintaining at other times, that neither praise nor blame, servitude or exile, being things foreign to a man's self, ought to give him any uneasiness.

Marcus Antoninus himself expresses, though somewhat obscurely, his approbation of self murder. "If you must die (Lib. v. sect. 29.) let it "be as those who have suffered nothing. If the "smoke be troublesome, I leave it. Why should "this appear of consequence to any person? But "nothing compels me to depart. I remove freely, since no person can hinder me from doing "what I please. It is my wish to do what belongs "to a man endued with reason, and born for society."

"ty." This allusion to his quitting a smoky house, looks like a voluntary act; the compulsion being very inconsiderable, since a smoky house is tolerable though not pleasant.

The amount of all these philosophical remedies against the fear of death, is nothing more than a patient acquiescence in what is unavoidable, and what must be taken for granted is right, with respect to the whole system of which we are a part: death, as well as birth, being included in it. The same argument applies to the deprivation of any thing that men value, as health, riches, pleasure, power, &c. &c. but what can prevent our regret at the loss of them, if we really value them? and is not life a thing that all men value, and consequently must they not naturally part with it, as well as other things, with regret, when they can retain it no longer, and have no prospect of any equivalent for the loss, which must have been the case with the heathen world? This is certainly the language of nature; and if philosophers say any thing to the contrary, as the Stoics do, it is a proof that their principles are not agreeable to nature, and therefore false, and their topics of consolation under affliction, and in the prospect of death, are not adapted to the nature and condition of man.

How

How unspeakably more natural, and therefore more efficacious, and valuable, is the consolation that christianity holds out to a dying man, who is conscious that he has lived a virtuous life! It is not the gloomy consolation of the dispersion of the elements of which his body consists, and never to be collected again, or the re-union of his soul to that of the whole universe, from which he cannot conceive any source of joy to himself individually, and of which, indeed, he cannot form any distinct idea; but the exchange of this life for a better, a state in which he will not be subject to sickness or pain, and in which he will not die any more, but continue in existence without end; and this not mere existence, but a life of the truest enjoyment, the enjoyment of things which the apostle says, *eye hath not seen, nor ear heard, and such as it has not entered into the mind of man to conceive*. With this prospect, certain and glorious, though not distinct and particular, well may the christian say in dying, *O death where is thy sting, O grave where is thy victory!* That christians of every denomination actually believe this, and that this is the most essential and unquestionable article of their faith, cannot be denied; and this firm faith accounts, in the most satisfactory manner, not only for the calm

calm resignation, which is all that the Stoics pretend to, but the joy with which thousands of christians have met death, and even endured the greatest tortures that could be inflicted upon them, rather than renounce their faith.

Had Marcus Antoninus been acquainted with the sentiments of christians on this subject, he could not have called their refusal to live on the terms that he proposed to them *obstinacy*, because it had a natural and real foundation, the bearing of an evil of short continuance, however severe, for a degree of happiness that would be an abundant re compence for it.

The Stoics, indeed, held out as we have seen a kind of immortality to man, in those great revolutions, to which they supposed that, at certain periods, every thing in nature would be subject, so that as every thing had once been in the very state in which it now is, it will sometime hence revert to the very same, and so without end, and without any improvement. But besides that this notion, which is also entertained by the Hindoos, and probably came into Greece from the East, is destitute of all foundation, and could hardly be seriously believed by any man, how inferior is it to that kind of immortality that christians are taught to

expect.

expect! A state of existence that will not only have no end, but that will be continually improving; an idea most sublime and transporting, and which is countenanced even by present appearances, as we actually observe the state of mankind, and of every thing we see, to be in a state of improvement.

Compared with the cold indifference, (and this no doubt in a great measure affected) with which Marcus Antoninus speaks of meeting death, how short does it fall of the joy, and even rapture, with which the apostle Paul speaks of his approaching end! (2. Tim. c. iv. v. 6.) *I am now ready to be offered, and the time of my departure is at hand. I have fought the good fight. I have finished my course. I have kept the faith. Henceforth there is laid up for me a crown of righteousness, which the Lord, the righteous judge, shall give me at that day; and not to me only, but unto all them also that love his appearing.* What an idea does this give us of the infinite superiority of the principles of christianity to those of heathen philosophy of every kind!

The probability is, that Marcus Antoninus held the christians (few of whom pretended to any knowledge of philosophy) in too great contempt to make any proper inquiry into their sentiments, or to read

read their writings. He had learned, he says, (Lib. i. sect. 6.) "of Diognetus not to spend his "time about trifles, nor to give credit to those who "dealt in inchantments and exorcisms, and other "impostures of that nature." And being under the influence, as he evidently was, of the Greek philosophers, and taking all his lessons from them, he was no doubt, taught to believe that all the miracles the christians pretended to, as the foundation of their religion, were no better founded than such inchantments and exorcisms as many of the heathens also pretended to.

So educated and instructed, he could not have any proper idea of the firm faith and hope of christians, which, without any aid of speculative philosophy, enabled them to bear, with what he calls *obstinacy*, all the tortures that he, in so unrelenting a manner, ordered to be inflicted upon them. What could his boasted philosophy do in comparison with this? Thus was the *wisdom of this world*, with every advantage that time and reflection could give it, mere *foolishness*, as the apostle called it, compared with the simple doctrines of christianity, which were intelligible and efficacious with the lowest, and least exercised understanding, as well as the highest. Indeed, the admirable plainness, and

as

as well as superior excellence of its principles, levels all distinctions of this and of every other kind. *To the poor the gospel is preached*, as well as to the rich; and it is equally intelligible to them. According to the gospel, as in the eye of God, all men are equal. It is conferred as a common blessing on all his offspring of mankind.

But with this excellent religion Marcus Antoninus was unacquainted, and from his pride as a philosopher, which is sufficiently conspicuous in his writings, his contempt of the *new doctrine* of christians, who made no account of his philosophy, or any other, his zeal for the welfare of the empire, at the head of which he was placed, and on which his glory depended, which, with all other heathens, he imagined to have some unknown connection with the observance of those antient rites, in which the christians refused to join, he might, without any particular cruelty in his disposition, direct the persecution which continued during the whole of his reign. It is farther probable that he only heard of the sufferings of the christians through the unfavourable accounts of his officers, who would naturally be disposed to ridicule, and make light of them, and to flatter him with respect to the success of his measures. And thus, without

out hearkening to any remonstrance or intreaty, and resisting, as his philosophy taught him to do, every motion of *compassion*, which he might think was farther unbecoming him as an emperor, he might persist as he did without remorse, in those rigorous proceedings as long as he lived. He had less knowledge of christianity than Julian, and therefore less guilt; as in all respects he was a much superior character.

THE PHILOSOPHY *of* ARRIAN AND SENECA.

INTRODUCTION.

SENECA and Arrian were both men of the world, and statesmen; the former tutor to Nero, and the latter distinguished by the most honourable employments under Adrian, and the succeeding emperors. But both of them were great writers, and both made profession of the Stoic philosophy. Arrian was a disciple of Epictetus, and the *Enchiridion* was composed by him from the sayings of his master. Seneca appears to have been well acquainted with all the sects of the Greek philosophy, and he particularly quotes a great number of the sayings of Epicurus, but he preferred the philosophy of the Stoics to any other.

"Others," he says (De Const. Sap. c. 1.) "proceed in a gentle manner, but the Stoics endea-

"your

"vour to raise men at once to the highest pitch "of excellence." This philosophy, indeed, may be said to have been the greatest effort of human genius on the important subject of *religion and morals*, in which the proper conduct of life, under all the evils of it, and the prospect of death, subjects so highly interesting to all men, are particularly insisted upon. I have, however, chosen to give the details of it from Marcus Antoninus and Epictetus, rather than from Seneca or Arrian, because the former, not being writers by profession, as we may consider the others to have been, may be supposed to have expressed their sentiments without exaggeration; so that we are in less danger of being misled by any thing like oratory in their works. Some valuable illustrations, however, of the Stoical principles will be found in the writings of Seneca and Arrian, and expressed with more emphasis, for which we may make what allowance we think proper.

SECTION I.

Of God and Providence.

The Stoics strictly followed Socrates in the belief of the being, and of the wise and benevolent providence, of a supreme intelligence, whether it resided in one subject or many. Indeed, on this all their distinguishing maxims, especially that of the soul of man being a portion of this intelligence, and retaining its powers, depended. Other philosophers held various opinions on this subject. Arrian gives the following account of them.

"Concerning the gods," he says, (Lib. i. cap. 12.) "some say there are no gods; others that they "exist, but take no care of any thing; others that "they exist, but take no care of any besides ce-"lestial things; others that they attend both to "celestial and terrestrial things, but only in a gene-"ral way; others, like Ulysses and Socrates, say "that we cannot even move without God." Arrian himself proves the being of a god from the wonderful frame of the world (Lib. i. cap. 6.) He even supposes that God made the *sun*, which Marcus Antoninus, and the heathens in general, supposed to be itself a deity. "Can that God who "made the sun, and guides it," he says (Lib. i. cap. 14.) "a small part of his works compared to "the universe, not see all things." Seneca also says (Ep. 41.) "such a system as this could not "stand without the support of the deity. When "you are most alone," says Arrian (Lib. i. cap.

cap. 14.) "God is within you; your geni- "us is within you. Do they require light to "see what you do?" See also Seneca, (Ep. 41.)

Like Socrates, the Stoics connected good morals with their regard to God. Arrian having mentioned the deity says (Lib. ii. cap. 14.) "such "as the deity is, such will be those who endea- "vour to please him. If he be faithful, they will "be so. If he be beneficent, they will be so. If he "be magnanimous, they will be so." He shews at large the great danger that would not fail to result to society from a general neglect of religion. "Then," says he (Lib. ii. cap. 20.) "justice is "nothing, modesty is folly, and the relation of fa- "ther and son is as nothing."

The constant presence, and assistance, of God was thought by some of the Stoics to be necessary to all good men. "There is no good man," says Seneca (Ep. 41.) "without God. No person can "rise above fortune, but as assisted by him. It is "he that gives great and exalted councils. God," he says, "removes from good men every evil, all "wickedness, evil thoughts, blind lust, avarice," &c. (De Provid. chap. 6.) He did not, however, suppose that the divine guide of each particular person was a deity of the highest rank. For he says (Ep. 110.) "Every person has a god for his "guide, but one of an inferior kind."*

The union of this intelligent principle, which occasionally descended to the earth to the aid of men, is thus expressed by Seneca (Ep. 41.) "As "the rays of the sun reach to the earth, but are "still united to their source; so a great and sa- "cred mind, being sent down hither that we may "have a nearer view of divine things, converses "with us, but adheres to its original."

It is not easy to say what the heathen philosophers and others thought of *fate*, and the relation that the gods bore to it. Sometimes they seem to have thought that they directed fate, at other times that fate was a power independent of them, and that controlled them. Seneca seems to have thought that fate was nothing more than the will of the gods themselves. "The author and governor of all things" he says (Prov. v. cap. 1.) "wrote the fates, but "he follows them. He orders, but always obeys. "Some things must always please God (Quæst. "Nat. Lib. i. præf.) because the best things "only please him. Nor is he on this account less "free,

* *Those of this class of deities that attended women were by the heathens called* Juno's.

"free, or powerful; for he is his own necessity. "If this be not the case, it would not be worth "while to be born."

It was taken for granted by all the later philosophers, that the gods were incapable of *anger*, as well as all good men; and the natural consequence of this opinion was that there could be no future punishment for the wicked, which took away a great motive against the commission of vice. "The immortal gods," says Seneca (De Ira. Lib. ii. c. 27.) "neither will any anger, nor can indulge "in any. Their nature is mild, and placid, as re- "mote from injuring others as themselves. No "man in his senses" he says (De Benef. Lib. iv. cap. 19.) "fears God, for it is madness to fear "what is salutary; nor can any person love what "he fears. No person is so much a child as to be "afraid of Cerberus." And he joins the Epicureans in their contempt of every thing in the infernal regions. (Ep. 24.)

It appears from the writings of Arrian, that the common people among the heathens were very religious in their way. "No person," he says (Lib. iii. cap. 21.) "leaves a port without sacrificing to "the gods; nor do husbandmen sow without in-

"voking Ceres. Would any person who should "neglect such duties be safe?"

He must have thought, however, that such rites as these took the place of duties of more importance, when he said (Lib. ii. cap. 7.) "By means of un-"seasonable divination many duties are neglect-"ed."

Section II.

Of the Soul of Man, and its Power.

We have seen enough, it might be thought, of the consequences which the Stoics drew from their opinion of the derivation of the souls of men from the supreme intelligence, in ascribing to them similar powers, especially that of absolute self-sufficiency, and a total independence on every thing foreign to itself, even, on the body, to which it is, however, necessarily connected at present. But arrogant as is the language of Marcus Antoninus and Epictetus on the subject, it falls short of that of Seneca.

One obvious similarity between God and man is their relation to *matter*. "The place," says Seneca (Ep. 65.) "that God has in the world, the "mind

" mind has in man. He works upon matter, and " the mind upon the body." But he surely could not think that the supreme mind was as necessarily attached to the material system as to be affected by every thing that passes in it, as the mind is by the affections of the body; which, though it may make light of it, has no power to free itself. The union of the soul with the supreme intelligence, notwithstanding its present separation from it, is thus maintained by Seneca. "There is nothing," he says, (Ep. 92.) "improper in endeavouring to " ascend from whence we came. Why should " we not think there is something divine in a good " man, since he is part of God. The whole sys- " tem is one, and is God. We are his compani- " ons, and members of him."

To christians, who believe that there is an infinite difference between God and man; and his infinite superiority to us, notwithstanding our being said to be *made in his image*, and to resemble him in some respects, the language of Seneca respecting their equality is truly shocking. " A good " man," he says, (De Provid, chap. 1. & 2.) " dif- " fers from God only with respect to time. He is his " disciple, his emulator, and true offspring, whom " he educates with severity, to prepare him for

" himself; but no real evil can befal a good man. " God," he farther says (Ep. 73.) " is not superi- " or to man in happiness, but only in time; and " virtue is not greater for being of longer continu- " ance." What he says above of God training up good men to prepare them for himself is a truly fine sentiment, though connected with so much extravagance.

Seneca goes beyond Marcus Antoninus in his boasting of the all sufficiency of the mind of man with respect to happiness, and its independence on every thing foreign to itself. " It is," he says, (De Consol. ad. Helv. c. 5.) " in the power of eve- " ry man to make himself happy. With respect to himself," he says, " I assure you I am not unhap- " py, (miserum)," and, moreover, that I cannot be " so (Ib. c. 4.) If small things cannot affect a wise " man, (De Constant. Sap. c. 15.) neither can " greater things; if not a few, neither many. I " would persuade you never to pity a good man, " De Prov. c. 3.) for though he may seem to be " miserable, he cannot be so."

To many this would seem a difficult attainment, but not so to our author. " What does reason " require of man, but the easiest things, (Ep. 41.) " viz. to live according to nature. A wise man is

" no

"no creature of imagination. There are many "examples of it, and Cato seems to have exceed- "ed what was required of him." (De Const. Sap. c. 7.

This extraordinary power, it is evident, however, that Arrian restricts to philosophers. "Philoso- "phy," says he, (Lib. ii. cap. 1.) "allows none to "be free, but those who have been instructed (πεπαι- "δευμενοι) that is, God does not permit it." Again he says, (Lib. ii. cap. 19.) "Shew me a person "who is sick and happy, in danger and happy, "dying and happy, banished and happy, disgraced "and happy, such a one is a Stoic." But, surely, such a one is rather a christian, his source of consolation under the evils mentioned alone, being infinitely superior to any that the Stoics could have recourse to, and accessible to persons of the meanest capacity, such as they could never have adopted, or indeed have understood, viz. the distinction of things within the power of the mind, and things foreign to it, in the sense of the Stoics. As to dying circumstances, there cannot, surely, be a question of the superior happiness of the christian, for reasons obvious enough, and enlarged upon in the preceding section.

"The

The power of the mind over the body is rather more strongly expressed by Arrian than by any other Stoic writer. "My body," he says, (Lib. iii. cap.) 22. "is not me, its parts are nothing to "me. Death is nothing to me, let it come when "it will." He supposes a dialogue between a tyrant and a philosopher that is truly curious for the extravagance of it. The tyrant says (Lib. i. cap. 1.) "You shall die." The philosopher replies, "but "not lamenting. T. You shall be in chains. P. "But not whining. T. You shall be banished. "P. But what hinders my going laughing. T. "Tell me your secrets. P. No, that is in my "power. T. But I will throw you into chains. "P. What say you, man? You may bind my "feet, but Jupiter himself cannot change my reso-"lution. T. I will throw you into prison, and "strike off your head. P. And did I ever say "that you could not strike it off? T. I will kill "you. P. When did I say that I was immortal? "These things," he says, "must be thought of, "and meditated upon."

In one place, however, Arrian seems willing to make some allowance for the weakness of human nature, and especially on account of the necessary influence of the body over the mind. "If the "gods,"

"gods," he says, (Lib. i. cap. 1.) "were willing "to grant us the command of the things that are "out of our power, they could not do it.. For "while we are upon the earth, and are tied to such "bodies, and such companions, how is it possible "but that things foreign to us must be an impedi-"ment to us."

Seneca, whose luxurious and splendid mode of living did but ill correspond with the maxims of his philosophy, and whose flattery of the emperor, whom he must have despised, was fulsome in the extreme, seems disposed to make still more allowance for the weakness of human nature than any other of the Stoics. "I would prefer pleasure," he says, (Ep. 66.) "to pain if the choice was "proposed to me, because the former is more a-"greeable to nature, and the latter contrary to it." But for the very same reason, is not every thing that men call *good* more agreeable to nature, than those that we agree to call *evils;* and how, on this concession, could pleasure and pain be classed among the things that are perfectly indifferent to a philosopher?

When his luxurious life was objected to him, he said, after reciting the particulars of it. "These "things are *apud me*, (in my possession) but at "the

"the same time they are *extra me*, (foreign to me, "i. e. to my mind") (De Vita. beata. cap. 25.) a "pretty nice, but convenient distinction." According to him, a more ingenious acknowledgment was made by Plato and Epicurus, when the same objection was made to them. For they said, "that men should live according to what they "thought, not as they themselves lived." (Ib 18.) It is not probable, however, that either of these men would have said this in earnest. Others may have said it for them, as Jesus did of the Scribes and Pharisees.

Section III.

Of Moral Precepts.

Arrian has many excellent moral precepts; but as they are similar to those of Marcus Antoninus above recited, they need not be repeated here. Among other things he says, (Lib. ii. cap. 6.) "Life "is a thing indifferent, but not so the use of it. "Difficulties shew who are men. When you "meet with them (Lib. i. cap. 24.) remember "that God is making you engage with a rough and "expert antagonist."

As

As the Stoics made no allowance for the indulgence of any *passion*, or *emotion*, which they referred to mere animal nature, they equally condemned *anger* and *compassion*. "Anger," says Seneca (De Ira ii. cap. 14.) "is never to be indulged, but "only the appearance of it to excite others as a "spur to a horse. A good man (Ib. 6.) is inca-"pable of inflicting punishment; but anger is a "punishment, and therefore anger it not natural." On this subject, as well as on every other how much more natural is the doctrine of the scriptures, which aims not at the extirpations of any of our passions, but only at the due regulation of them. *Be ye angry, but sin not. Let not the sun go down upon your wrath.* "Compassion," he says (Clem. ii. cap. 4.) "is a vice of the mind, "in the view of the miseries of others. A wise "man will relieve a person that weeps, but he will "not weep with him (cap. 6.) He will relieve the "distressed, but without feeling compassion."

On the subject of *self murder* Arrian seems to be inconsistent. "God," he says (Lib. i. cap. 29.) "requires such a world as this, and those that are "in it. If he order a retreat, as in the case of So-"crates, we should yield obedience, as to a com-

"mander

"mander in chief." But on another occasion he supposes that men have a right to judge for themselves in this case, without waiting for the orders of any superior. Addressing a discontented person he says, (Lib.i. cap. .9) "You slave, if you be "not satisfied, go out of life. The gate is open."

Seneca is quite decided in favour of the latter opinion. "If you dislike life," he says (De Prov. c. 6.) the door is open. If you will not fight, you "may fly." He frequently commends Cato for putting an end to his own life: He even says (Ep. 13.) "Take away the sword from Cato, and you "take from him a great part of his glory."

The indifference that he expressed to life or death would appear affected, as his language certainly is on other occasions, but that he actually did meet death with sufficient fortitude, at the command of a cruel and capricious tyrant. "Death," he says (Ep. 24.) "is so far from being to be feared, that "nothing is to be preferred to the benefit to be de-"rived from it." Lipsius, however, proposes another reading) which softens this. He also says (Ep. 54.) "We know what death is. It is to be "what we were before we were born, when we "had no sense of *evil.*" But it follows from this that neither shall we have after death a sense of any *good.*

good. And this seems to have been the real opinion of all the later heathen philosophers, notwithstanding what they sometimes say of the immortality of the soul. When, in his eloquent manner, he describes the destruction and renovation of the world he says (De Consolatione ad Marciam. cap. 26.) "We also, happy souls, when it "shall please God to renew all things, shall only "be a small addition to the immense ruin, and "shall be changed into the antient elements."

What he says to Marcia, (cap. 25.) of her son being received by the Scipio's and Cato's; &c. after his death, could only be said by way of accommodation to her opinion, and as a topic of consolation, and not his own real belief.

THE PHILOSOPHY *of* EPICURUS.

INTRODUCTION.

THE only sect of Grecian philosophy that remains to be considered, as coming within my object, of a comparison of them with the system of revelation, is that of *Epicurus* which arose presently after that of the Stoics, to which it was, in many respects, opposite and hostile; the one being remarkable for its austerity, and the other for its ease in the conduct of life; the one for a belief in a divine providence, as superintending every thing in the world, and the other for the utter neglect and contempt of religion in every form. There was also another source of opposition and hostility between the two. All the philosophers who had preceeded Epicurus, the Stoics among the rest, had deserted the plain maxims of Socrates, and spent the

the greatest part of their time on Logic and Metaphysicks, of no use whatever in the conduct of life; whereas Epicurus, following the steps of their common master, held all their subtle disputations on these subjects in the greatest contempt, and made the true enjoyment of life the great object of his philosophy. And considering that the great doctrine of a future state was in fact excluded from all their systems, there was more of reason and good sense in the maxims of Epicurus than in theirs; especially as, though he maintained that pleasure was the great end of life, he did not, as we shall see, mean sensual pleasure, but the happiness of man upon the whole, in which temperance, and every virtue, was an essential ingredient.

Epicurus also differed from other philosophers in the circumstances of his teaching, more resembling a society of friends, than that of master and scholars. Their meetings were held in a private garden of his own; and the friendship of this fraternity Cicero spake of in the highest terms. (Acad. Lib. 20.) though they had not every thing in common, like the disciples of Pythagoras.

Though we have no proper *treatise* of Epicurus, we have several of his *letters* preserved by Diogenes Laertius, especially one to Herodotus, in which he professes to give an outline of his principles. And the poem of Lucretius contains a developement of the whole of his philosophy. From these it is easy to form a very complete idea of his tenets; and from these, and some of his sayings quoted by Seneca, the following account is given.

Section I.

Of God and of the Structure of the Universe.

Epicurus's triumph over religion in all its forms, and thereby delivering men from the fear of death, was the great boast of all his followers, this victory (Lucretius says Lib. i. V. 78.) has raised men from earth to heaven, and by this means he has conferred greater benefit on mankind than Ceres in giving them bread, or Bacchus in giving them wine (Ib. Lib. v. V. 15.) Religion he considered as having done unspeakable mischief to mankind, and in particular instances the sacrifice of Iphigenia, the daughter of Agamemnon to Diana, of which he gives a very affecting description. (Lucret. Lib. i. V. 85.)

Epicurus did not, however deny the existence of gods, and though this is commonly thought to have

have been only with a view to his safety; since by an open profession of atheism he would have been exposed to the rigour of the Athenian laws, I think he might have been very sincere in that opinion; thinking, with all other philosophers, that every part of the universe was replete with inhabitants, suited to their natures, the gods occupying the higher regions, demons the middle, and men the earth. What he openly maintained was that, tho' there are gods they take no thought about the affairs of this world. "The gods," he says (Diog. Laert. pag. 785.) "are immortal "and happy beings *** but not such as the "vulgar opinion makes them to be;" and having said that happiness is two fold, he adds that "supreme happiness is that of the gods which ad-"mits of no addition." (Ib 783-4.)

The reason that he gives for this opinion is, that happiness could not consist with the trouble and care which he thought must attend the government of the world, though he seems to have thought that they had something to do in the upper regions, which are nearest to them. Speaking of the motions, and other properties of meteors, he says (Ib. 755.) "They are not directed by any "thing besides the order and appointment of him

"who

" who has all happiness and immortality. For it " is inconsistent with happiness to have business, " and cares, or to be affected by anger, or favour, " These belong to beings subject to infirmity, and " fear, who stand in need of others." Again he says, (Ib. 735.) " Whoever is happy, and immor" tal, neither has any troublesome business him" self, nor gives trouble to others; and in conse" quence of this he is neither moved by anger " or favour."

As to the charge of impiety he says, (Ib. 786.) " he is not guilty of impiety who takes from the " multiplicity of Gods, but he who adopts the opi" nion of the multitude concerning them," Lucretius ascribes the origin, and the frightful effects of religion upon the human mind, in part to what people see, or imagine they see, in dreams, as well as to the irregular course of the heavenly bodies, and to the terror excited by storms, thunder, lightning, earthquakes, &c. For seeing no cause of these things, men ascribe them to some unknown invisible beings, whose power was great, and tremendous. (Lucret. Lib. v. V. 1165. &c.

Considering the vulgar superstition. and the serious effects of it in human sacrifices. prostituti-

ons

ons in religious rites, divination, and its distructing influence in the common business of life, it may well be questioned whether it was not wiser, with Epicurus, to reject it altogether, than to retain it in any form or degree. Nay I doubt not but the system of Polytheism and Idolatry took more from the happiness of mankind than either Epicurus or Lucretius suspected. Epicurus, however, well knew that none of the philosophers maintained the vulgar opinions, but much more honourable ideas of the divinity and the government of the world, opinions highly pleasing to good men, and perhaps some restraint upon the wicked; and we shall see that his ideas of the government of the world, and the direction of it, which differed exceedingly from those of other philosophers, were absurd in the extreme, in supposing that there was no wisdom, design, or a regard to final causes, in things that most of all required them.

The Atomical system, which was opposed to that of Plato, and most other philosophers, who held that the world was formed by an intelligent principle, out of pre-existent matter, and that it was finite, was first suggested by Democritus, but adopted by Epicurus. He maintained that there was no wisdom employed in the arrangement of any part of the system, but that it arose from the fortuitous concourse of atoms, moving at random in all directions. "These atoms" he says, (Diog. Laert. p. 741.) "have no properties besides those "of figure, gravity and magnitude; but being "perfectly hard, though of different forms, they "are incapable of destruction, or change." The construction of the world, according to Lucretius, is too faulty to have arisen from a principle of intelligence and design. (Lucret. Lib. ii. V. 180.)

The universe having come into existence from these materials, "it must." Epicurus says (Ib. 733.) "be infinite. For had there been any bounds "to it, the parts of which it consists would have "been dispersed into infinite space; having no "place to fix in, and nothing to stop their motion," moreover, since the giving these floating atoms every chance for their fortunate meeting, so as to form such a compleate system as this, must have required almost infinite time before it could have taken place, he maintained, contrary to the opinion of many other philosophers that "the world had a "beginning, and will have an end. (Lib. v. V. 245.) Since the continual contention, and disposition to motion, in the elements of which it consists will in course of time effect its compleat dissolution

solution. He even thought there were already evident signs of a tendency to decay and dissolution in the earth, and that there has been a great degeneracy in all its productions, animals being now of less size and strength than they were formerly, and all the products of the earth requiring the labour of man which they did not originally, when every thing for the use of man was produced by it spontaneously (Lucret. Lib. ii. V. 1150. and 1170.) so that in time every thing will probably decline more and more, and the whole go to decay and ruin. But since nothing could be formed out of nothing, the atoms of which it consists can only be dispersed to form other systems, and can never be annihilated (Lucret. Lib. i. V. 150. & 216.) But before this event takes place Epicurus maintained that, with the exception of the gradual decay mentioned above, "every thing is now as it "ever has been, and will continue to be; since there is nothing into which it can be changed, and no superior power to make a change in it. (Diog. Laert. p. 732.)

In the same manner as this world was formed, viz. by the random concourse of atoms, since the universe has no bounds, "other worlds," Epicurus says (Diog. Laert. p. 735. and 736.) "have, "no doubt been formed in the same manner; and "there is no reason why there may not be an in- "finity of them, similar or dissimilar to this. "For the atoms of which they are composed are "infinite, and carried to the greatest distances."

Such wild and absurd schemes, altogether unworthy of examination or refutation, may the most ingenious of men be led to form for want of attention to a few fundamental principles, and those of the most obvious nature. For what can be more evident than that there are infinite marks of design, and what we call contrivance, in the structure of the world, and of every plant and animal in it. Epicurus must have maintained that the eye was not formed for seeing, nor the ear for hearing; but that being so formed, by this fortuitous concourse of atoms, they were found to be capable of these particular uses. Other philosophers, however, were not backward to acknowledge the reality of final causes, and consequently of design in the structure of the world, and of every part of it, and it is certainly unspeakably more satisfactory to acknowlede, than to deny, this. We have then some superior intelligence to look to, as a being to whom this world, and ourselves as a part of it, belong; and who will take some care of what

with

with such exquisite skill, he has planned and executed.

SECTION II.

Of the Human Soul.

Since, according to Epicurus, every thing is in a perpetual flux, through the constant tendency to motion in its primary atoms, it could not be supposed that he would, with many other philosophers, maintain either the *pre-existence*, or the *immortality* of the soul. Accordingly he denies, and even ridicules, them both; using however one just argument, though he was little aware of the real nature or extent of it, viz. "All thought arises from the impression made on the bodily senses," (Diog. Laert. p. 727.) thinking it to follow from this, that the soul, on which the impressions were made, was equally corporeal with the objects from which they came.

His principal argument, however, is that there is nothing in nature besides *body* and *space*, in which bodies can be placed, and moved. "There "is nothing," he says (Ib. 732) "but what can "be handled," or become the object of our senses.

ses." "We cannot even form an idea of any thing "else. Nothing," he says, (Ib. 749.) "is incor- "poreal," (which all other philosophers held the soul to be) "besides a *vacuum*, which only affords "room for bodies to move in." He adds "they "who say that the soul is incorporeal talk fool- "ishly. (ματαιάζουσι)"

The soul, then, being corporeal, must be a part of the body, as much as the hands or the feet (Lucret. Lib. iii. v. 95.) each having their several functions; and as the soul had no pre-existence, it must have been produced at the same time with the body, grow up, and decay, with it. (Lucret. Lib. iii. v. 455.). Being a body, it must consist of particles of some particular kind or form, and "those that constitute the soul," he says, (Diog. Laert. p. 747.) "are the smallest and roundest of "all; but they must be dispersed when the body "dies, as every other part of it is." (Ib. 748.)

It is difficult to form any clear or consistent idea of Epicurus's opinion concerning the different parts of the soul, of their several functions, and place in the body. In his letter to Herodotus he mentions only two parts, one that has reason, and another that is destitute of it. "The rational "part,"

"part," he says (Ib. 748.) "resides in the breast, "as is manifest from the passions of fear and joy." But, according to Lucretius, there are three, or even four parts in the soul; and yet when he speaks of three parts, he mentions only the *Animus* and the *Anima;* but the third seems to be the *breath* which leaves us when we die. (Lucret. Lib. iii. V. 231. to 245.) Afterwards, however, he says that these three parts are not sufficient, but that "a fourth which has no name must be added, and "this is the cause of universal sensation; though, "like the other parts, it consists of the smallest par-"ticles of matter." (Lucret. Lib. iii V. 236.) That *heat* enters into the composition of the soul, appears, he says, (Lucret. Lib. iii. V. 290.) when we are angry, and in the habits of fierce animals, as lions, &c. and that *air* is another part of it, appears when we are cool and serene, and in the cold dispositions of the deer, and tame animals.

Since the soul, according to Epicurus, is not immortal, death must be the extinction of our being; and the dread of this is represented by him and Lucretius as the greatest of all evils, and what most of all tends to embitter human life, as it must to those who have any enjoyment of it, and have nothing

nothing to look to beyond it. "Take a young "man," he says, as he is quoted by Seneca (Ep. 22.) "an old man, or one of middle age, you will "find them equally afraid of dying, though equal-"ly ignorant of life." In order to relieve the mind from this terror, he says with other philosophers, (Ib. 786.) "Accustom yourself to think "that death is nothing to us. For both good and "evil consist in sensation, and death is a privation "of all sense." Again he says, (Ib. 786.) "death, "the most dreadful of all evils, is nothing to us; "because while we live death is not present, and "when death comes we are not." This poor witticism is not, however, calculated to give much consolation to a man who is sensible of the approach of death, and who is unwilling to part with life.

There are two sentences of Epicurus concerning death, preserved by Seneca, which have more of good sense in them. "It is," he says (Ep 24.) "ridiculous to fly to death through a wearisome-"ness of life, after living in such a manner as that "death is the only and the last resource." Again (Ep. 26.) "Think whether it is more desira-"ble for death to come to us, or for us to go to it; "that is, since death will come, it is better to meet

"it

"it cheerfully." But in vain are all the topics of consolation against the fear of death to men who love life, and yet have no hope of surviving the grave, and this hope is no where given but in revelation.

Section III.

Of Human Life and Happiness.

Admitting what, in fact, all the Grecian philosophers did, viz. that there is no future state, the maxims of Epicurus respecting this life, and the proper objects of choice in it, are far more reasonable than those of any of the other sects. Since (as he insinuates) there is no life beyond this, "It "is," he says (Diog. Laert. p. 758.) "our bu-"siness to make the most of the things that are "present, and exclude all causes of anxiety. The "end of all," he says, (Ib. 788.) "is to live well, "and happily. For we do every thing to avoid "grief and perturbation." He therefore adds, (Ib. 789.) that "pleasure is the end and object of "life, but not all kinds of pleasure. For some "we decline because they are all attended with "more pain, and some pains we chuse for the sake "of "of the pleasures that follow them. Perturbati-"on," he says, (Ib. 758.) "is incident to men in "this life, especially to those who dread what, ac-"cording to fabulous accounts, we may meet with "after death, as if there was any thing after death. "But by living without perturbation we live," he says, (Ib. 759.) "as gods among men." For this we have seen to be his idea of the state of the gods.

It is probable that Epicurus was led by natural inclination to a quiet unambitious life. This he thought to be most favourable to the true enjoyment of it, and therefore he recommended it to others, and advised them to avoid whatever might interfere with it. "A wise man," he says (Ib. 782.) "will marry and have children, but he will "have no concern in public affairs." This was probably to avoid every jealousy and opposition, with all the unpleasant consequences of them, unavoidable to men in public life. For it could not be from idleness, in a man who wrote so many books, and who employed so much of his time in the instruction of others. From a similar motive he might say, (Ib. 784.) "A wise man will make "use of poems, but will not compose any him-"self." Agreeably to this he says, (Ib. 761.) "the

" the happiness of life does not require vanity, or " vain glory," which he might think to be particularly conspicuous in poets, " but in tranquility " and security."

In order to secure his favourite tranquility, he recommended the practice of universal virtue; and according to all accounts, his own life was without reproach in this respect. " The virtues," he says, (Ib. 795.) " are chosen for the sake of pleasure, " and not on their own account;" which is true when properly explained. For when the two are compared, happiness appears to be the *end*, and virtue the *means*, though the necessary means, to attain it.

He justly represents the chief cause of perturbation, and consequently of unhappiness in general, to be wrong dispositions of mind, which he says it is the business of philosophy to correct. " What " men suffer," he says, (Ib. 781.) " from hatred, " envy or contempt, a man may overcome by rea- " son; and he who has once been wise will not " acquire different habits, or yield to any cause of " perturbation, or to any thing else that may retard " his progress in knowledge. A wise man," he says, (Ib. 784.) " will not be affected if another be "said to be wiser than he." On this account he recommends an application to philosophy at all times of life. "If any person say it is too soon or too "late to apply to philosophy, it is, he says, the same "thing as if he said it is too late or too soon to be "happy." (Ib. 785.)

The life of Epicurus was according to all accounts conformable to his precepts; and so far was he or his disciples from habits of self-indulgence, that no persons lived more abstemiously, on the plainest food, and drinking little besides water. (Ib. 713.) What he himself says on this subject, (Ib. 790.) is particularly deserving of attention.

"We consider frugality," he says, "as a great "good, not that we should always live sparingly, "but that when we cannot do otherwise, we may "be satisfied with a little, and have a greater en-"joyment of abundance when we have it. Plain "bread and water give the greatest pleasure when "they are wanted; and to accustom ones'self to "plain food, not exquisitely prepared, contri-"butes both to health and activity for all the pur-"poses of life, and makes us not to dread bad for-"tune. When, therefore, we say that pleasure is "the end of life, it is not the pleasure of the luxu-"rious and the spendthrift, which consists in eat-

"ing

" ing and drinking to excess, which come, through " ignorance or perverseness, say that we maintain, " but to be free from pain of body and to enjoy " tranquility of mind, free from all perturbation. " There is no living pleasantly but by living pru- " dently, honorably, and justly. For the virtues " are connected with a delightful and pleasant life, " and cannot be seperated from them." Epicurus must have been of a pleasant, social, and benevolent turn of mind, to have attached so many persons to him as is universally acknowledged that he did. He says, (Ib. 801.) " the most valuable " thing in life is the acquisition of friendship."

I shall conclude this article with some valuable sayings of Epicurus, quoted by Seneca. " If you " live according to nature, you will never be poor, " but if you live according to the opinion of others, " you will never be rich (Ep. 10.) The man " who lives upon bread and water can never be " poor; and he who can confine his desires to " this, may vie with Jupiter for happiness (Ep. 25.) " First consider with whom you eat and drink; " and then what you eat and drink (Ep. 19.) They " live ill who are always beginning to live." (Ep. 23.)

Thus we have seen that, at the commencement

of our enquiry, all the more intelligent Greeks retained the belief of the existence of one Supreme Being, the maker of the world, and of all things in it, though aided by a multiplicity of inferior ones in the government of it: of the constant attention of this great Being to all human affairs, of his love of virtue, and abhorrence of vice, and of such an administration of the world, as that the wicked will generally meet with their due punishment, and the virtuous with their proper reward; that the souls of all men are immortal, and will be more fully rewarded or punished, according to their deserts, in a future state. But as we have advanced, we have found these principles and motives of moral conduct grow more obscure, till at last they entirely vanished; other principles, utterly inconsistent with them, being generally received; as that of the derivation of all human souls from the substance of the Supreme Being, and their final absorption into the same source again, all individual consciousness being thereby lost. The last of these sects, viz. that of the Epicureans, who discover more good sense, and consistency in other respects, disclaimed all belief of wisdom and design in the construction of the universe, and of the providence of God in any of the affairs of men at this

time

time, too, the last period of heathen philosophy, all the sects, without exception, had abandoned the belief of a future state of any kind. And yet, with respect to mental ability, the founders of these sects may be classed among the first of the human race, sagacious, thoughtful, and laborious, in the extreme. What prospect was there, then, of the world ever becoming more enlightened by human wisdom, and the experiment was continued a sufficient length of time, from Pythagoras to Marcus Antoninus, a space of about seven hundred years.

But what men could not do for themselves, it pleased God to do for them; and after giving much light to one particular nation, *in the fulness of time* he sent Jesus Christ, with abundant evidence of a divine mission to be the light of the whole world. His doctrine, in a reasonable time, through the instrumentality of men, to appearance the least qualified for the undertaking, and in spite of all opposition from power, from prejudice, and from heathen philosophy, establised itself, to the utter overthrow of all preceeding religions, which having been maintained from time immemorial, and thought to be connected with the well being of every state, had ever been held the most sacred.

cred. At present no doubt is entertained by any christian of the being or providence of God in this state, or of a righteous retribution in another; so that nothing is wanting, no *principle* or *motive*, whatever, to the virtue and happiness of man, but his receiving this divine light, and living according to it.

THE END.

DEDICATION.

To JOSHUA TOULMIN, D. D.

DEAR SIR,

MY having had for many years the happiness of your acquaintance and friendship, and particularly my having lately turned my thoughts to the subject of one of your valuable *dissertations*, have led me to take the liberty to address to you the following *Essay*, chiefly as a testimonial, and one of the last that I shall be able to give, of my esteem for your general principles and character.

Having here much leisure, and having been led to look back to some writings of the antients with which I was formerly much better acquainted than I am now, and among others the *Memorabilia of Xenophon*, and *Plato's account of Socrates*, it occurred to me to draw out an exhibition of his principles

ciples and conduct from the words of those two original writers; and this suggested the idea of drawing a comparison between him and Jesus. Knowing that you had published an excellent dissertation on the same subject, I forbore to look into it till mine was transcribed for the press. By this means I was not biassed, as I naturally should have been, in favour of your opinion; and I have seldom more than a very indistinct recollection of any work that I have not very recently read. On this second perusal of your Dissertation I was as much pleased with it as I remember I was at the first, though I found that in some particulars I differ from you. I hope that neither of us, inattentive as most persons now are to subjects of this kind, will have wholly written in vain.

I take this opportunity of publicly thanking you for your many excellent publications in defence of rational christianity. Having given so many specimens of your ability and zeal in the cause, it is to you, and your excellent coadjutors, Mr. Belsham, Mr. Kentish, and a few others, that the friends to the same cause will naturally look, whenever particular occasions, occurring on your side of the water, will appear to call for a champion. My labours in this or any other field of

exertion

exertion are nearly over; but it gives me much satisfaction to reflect on what I have done in defence of what appeared to me important christian truth. As we have *laboured*, I hope we shall hereafter *rejoice*, together. But we must *hold out to the end*, without being *weary of well doing*, indulging no remission of labour while we are capable of any. Even a dying hand has sometimes done execution. According to the apostle Paul, the whole life of every christian is *a warfare*. Our enemies are *vice* and *error*, and with them we must make neither peace nor truce. Their advocates will not make either peace or truce with us.

I know I shall not offend you by acknowledging, as I now do, that I had a particular view to *you* in my late tract in favour of *infant baptism*. Whatever you may think of the performance itself, you will not, I am confident, think uncandidly of the intention with which it was written. While we really think for ourselves, it is impossible, in this state at least, but that we must often see things in different lights, and consequently form different opinions concerning them. But with the ingenuous minds which become christians this will only be an occasion of exercising that candour

which

which is one of the most prominent christian virtues, in which I am persuaded you will never be defective.

With a very high degree of esteem,

I am,

Dear Sir,

yours sincerely.

J. PRIESTLEY.

Northumberland Jan. 1803.

Though the Dedication to Dr. Toulmin of that article in the work which relates to Socrates has no relation whatever to the subject of it, and is therefore not inserted at the head of that article in this publication, my father wishing to preserve it as a monument of their friendship, directed me to have it printed at the end of the whole work.

J. P.